MORE
TREASURY OF LOVE
POEMS, QUOTATIONS & PROVERBS
AVAILABLE:

Treasury of African Love
Treasury of Arabic Love
Treasury of Czech Love
Treasury of Finnish Love
*Treasury of French Love**
*Treasury of German Love**
Treasury of Hungarian Love
*Treasury of Irish Love**
*Treasury of Italian Love**
*Treasury of Jewish Love**
*Treasury of Polish Love**
Treasury of Love Poems by Adam Mickiewicz
Treasury of Roman Love
*Treasury of Russian Love**
*Treasury of Spanish Love**
Treasury of Ukrainian Love

* *Also available as an Audio Book*

HIPPOCRENE BOOKS
171 Madison Avenue • New York, NY 10016

Treasury of Indian Love

Poems & Proverbs from the Indian Sub-Continent

Edited by

CHRISTOPHER SHACKLE
& NICHOLAS AWDE

HIPPOCRENE BOOKS
NEW YORK

Acknowledgments

Graham Springett, Ron Asher, Stuart Blackburn, Mike Hutt, J. C. Wright, Ramesh Dogra & Rosemary Seton

ISBN 0-7818-0670-4

For information, address:
HIPPOCRENE BOOKS
171 Madison Avenue • New York, NY 10016

Printed in the United States of America

Contents

Proverbs of Love

SANSKRIT

Kisses classified

The passion-kindling kiss :
When she looks at his face while he sleeps and kisses it to show her desire.

The distracted kiss :
When she kisses him while he is inattentive or quarrelling or thinking of something else or sleepy.

The awakening kiss :
When someone comes late at night and to show his desire kisses his beloved who is asleep on the bed.
She may go on seeming to be asleep at the time of her lover's arrival in order to establish his inclinations.

The purposeful kiss :
When someone kisses the reflection of the beloved in a mirror, in water or on a wall.

The transferred kiss :
When someone kisses a child, a picture or a statue.

The challenging kiss :
When a man comes up to a woman at night in the theatre or at a party and kisses her on the fingers, or on the toes if she is sitting.
When a woman is massaging her lover and lays her head on his thigh as if overcome by sleep, and to arouse him kisses his thigh or his big toe.

And here there is a verse :

Each act in kind should be repaid
With stroke for stroke, and kiss for kiss

—*Vatsyayana : 'Kamasutra'*

❧ *A prose quotation from the world's most famous book of love, composed some 1,600 years ago* ❧

निशाः शशाङ्कक्षतनीलराजयः
क्वचिद्विचित्रं जलयन्त्रमन्दिरम् ।
मणिप्रकाराः सरसं च चन्दनं
शुचौ प्रिये यान्ति जनस्य सेव्यताम् ॥

सुवासितं हर्म्यतलं मनोहरं
प्रियामुखोच्छ्वासविकम्पितं मधु ।
सुतन्त्रिगीतं मदनस्य दीपनं
शुचौ निशीथेऽनुभवन्ति कामिनः ॥

नितम्बबिम्बैः सदुकूलमेखलैः
स्तनैः सहाराभरणैः सचन्दनैः ।
शिरोरुहैः स्नानकषायवासितैः
स्त्रियो निदाघं शमयन्ति कामिनाम् ॥

नितान्तलाक्षारसरागरञ्जितै-
र्नितम्बिनीनां चरणैः सनूपुरैः ।
पदे पदे हंसरुतानुकारिभि-
र्जनस्य चित्तं क्रियते समन्मथम् ॥

सचन्दनाम्बुव्यजनोद्भवानिलैः
सहारयष्टिस्तनमण्डलार्पणैः ।
सवल्लकीकाकलिगीतनिस्वनै-
र्विबोध्यते सुप्त इवाद्य मन्मथः ॥

सितेषु हर्म्येषु निशासु योषितां
सुखप्रसुप्तानि मुखानि चन्द्रमाः ।
विलोक्य निर्यन्त्रणमुत्सुकश्चिरं
निशाक्षये याति ह्रियेव पाण्डुताम् ॥

SANSKRIT

Hot summer nights

The dark nights broken by the moon
The fountain's cool and dome-shaped spray
The jewels and sweet sandalwood
Are summertime's delights, my dear.

The perfumed palace balconies
The wine-breath from a dear one's lips
The heart-felt songs set to the lute
Give lovers summer nights of joy.

With rounded bottoms clad in silk
With breasts bedecked with sandal paste
With fresh-washed, sweetly fragrant hair
The women soothe their lovers' heat.

Dyed crimson by the *lac*-tree's juice
Their feet are set with ankle-bells
Whose swan-like call at every step
Brings lovers under Cupid's rule.

By draughts from sandal-sprinkled fans
By pearls encircling rounded breasts
By rich sounds from the *veena*'s strings
The God of Love is roused from sleep.

All night the moon looks down in lust
Upon the women's faces whom
The palace's cool roof lets sleep
Until abashed by dawn he pales.

—*Kalidasa : 'Ritusamhara'*

❧ *From a poem on the favourite Indian theme of the 'seasons of love' by the great poet and dramatist Kalidasa (c. 400 AD)* ❧

मात्सर्यमुत्सार्य विचार्य कार्यमार्याः समर्यादमिदं वदन्तु ।
सेव्या नितम्बाः किमु भूधराणामुत स्मरस्मेरविलासिनीनाम् ॥

किमिह बहुभिरुक्तैर्युक्तिशून्यैः प्रलापै-
र्द्वयमिह पुरुषाणां सर्वदा सेवनीयम् ।
अभिनवमदलीलालालसं सुन्दरीणां
स्तनभरपरिखिन्नं यौवनं वा वनं वा ॥

नामृतं न विषं किंचिदेकां मुक्त्वा नितम्बिनीम् ।
सैवामृतलता रक्ता विरक्ता विषवल्लरी ॥

सन्मार्गे तावदास्ते प्रभवति च नरस्तावदेवेन्द्रियाणां
लज्जां तावद्विधत्ते विनयमपि समालम्बते तावदेव ।
भ्रूचापाकृष्टमुक्ताः श्रवणपथगता नीलपक्ष्माण एते
यावल्लीलावतीनां हृदि न धृतिमुषो दृष्टिबाणाः पतन्ति ॥

आवासः क्रियतां गाङ्गे पापहारिणि वारिणि ।
स्तनद्वये तरुण्या वा मनोहारिणि हारिणि ॥

वचसि भवति सङ्गत्यागमुद्दिश्य वार्ता
श्रुतिमुखरमुखानां केवलं पण्डितानाम् ।
जघनमरुणरत्नग्रन्थिकाञ्चीकलापं
कुवलयनयनानां को विहातुं समर्थः ॥

SANSKRIT

Love or renunciation ?

To which should we devote ourselves : the hermit's mountainside
Or else the rounded sensual forms of women built for love ?

❦

Just two things count in life : young heavy-breasted women
Who are made keen for sport by wine—or else the forest.

❀

All nectar and all venom too are broad-hipped women's gifts
Ambrosia in love but poison-ivy out of it.

❦

The righteous man may be the master of his senses till
A woman's arrow-glance wings from her eyes into his heart.

❀

Settle down beside the Ganges which cleanses all your sins
Or between a pair of breasts which blank out all your thoughts.

❦

Renouncing the world is fine as the subject of sermons
But who'll turn from the hips of fair women begirdled with rubies ?

—*Bhartrihari*

❧ *This seventh century collection of 100 verses on love explores the classic Indian tension between sensuality and asceticism* ❧

कथितसमयेऽपि हरिरहह न ययौ वनम् ।
मम विफलमिदममलरूपमपि यौवनम् ॥
यामि हे कमिह शरणं सखीजनवचनवञ्चिता ॥ ध्रुवम्

यदनुगमनाय निशि गहनमपि शीलितम् ।
तेन मम हृदयमिदमसमशरकीलितम् ॥ यामि हे०

मम मरणमेव वरमतिवितथकेतना ।
किमिह विषहामि विरहानलमचेतना ॥ यामि हे०

मामहह विधुरयति मधुरमधुयामिनी ।
कापि हरिमनुभवति कृतसुकृतकामिनी ॥ यामि हे०

अहह कलयामि वलयादिमणिभूषणम् ।
हरिविरहदहनवहनेन बहुदूषणम् ॥ यामि हे०

कुसुमसुकुमारतनुमतनुशरलीलया ।
स्रगपि हृदि हन्ति मामतिविषमशीलया ॥ यामि हे०

अहमिह निवसामि नगणितवनवेतसा ।
स्मरति मधुसूदनो मामपि न चेतसा ॥ यामि हे०

हरिचरणशरणजयदेवकविभारती ।
वसतु हृदि युवतिरिव कोमलकलावती ॥ यामि हे०

SANSKRIT

Where is he ?

He promised but where was he ?
My beauty's now quite useless
    Oh, who is there to help me ?
    My friends have all betrayed me.

To meet him in the forest
I went and I was wounded.

To die would be far better
Than suffering these feelings.

This sweet spring night torments me
Another woman's with him.

My jewels and bangles hurt me
I'm set on fire without him.

This garland, even, pains me
Strange symbol of love's arrow.

I wait lost in the jungle
Unthought of and forgottten.

    In Hari's name I utter
    This song to give you comfort.

—*Jayadeva : 'Gitagovinda'*

❧ *A song sung by Radha about Krishna from a famous 12th century poem* ❧

अवरण्हागयजामाउयस्स विउणेइ मोहणुक्कंठं
वहुयाए घरपरोहडमज्जणमुहलो वलयसद्दो ॥

वाउद्धयसिययविहाविओरुदिट्ठेण दंतमग्गेण ।
वहुमाया तोसिज्जइ निहाणकलसस्स व मुहेण ॥

उद्धंतमहारंभे थणए दट्ठूण मुद्धवहुयाए ।
ओसिन्नकवोलाए नीससियं पढमघरिणीए ॥

निव्वत्तरया वि वहू सुरयविरामट्ठिइं अयाणंती ।
अविरयहियया अन्नं पि किं पि अत्थि त्ति चिंतेइ ॥

सच्चं साहसु देवर तं तह चडुयारएण सुणएण ।
निव्वट्टियकज्जपरंमुहत्तणं सिक्खियं कत्तो ॥

तडविणिहियग्गहत्था वारितरंगेसु दोलिरणियंबा ।
सालूरी पडिबिंबे पुरिसायंति व्व पडिहाइ ॥

हेमंते हिमरयधूसरस्स असरणस्स पहियस्स ।
सुमरियजायामुहसिज्जिरस्स सीयं चिय पणट्ठं ॥

PRAKRIT

Thoughts of love-making

The young man at her parents' is further enflamed by the sound
Of the bangles she jingles so loud as she showers in their yard.

❦

Lifting her dress, the wind reveals the love-bites on her thighs
A glimpse of buried treasure to her mother, pleased she's loved.

❀

The young wife's firmly jutting breasts provoke
A sweat upon the sighing co-wife's cheeks.

❦

The young wife does not know how sex is meant to peak
Unsatisfied she thinks : there must be more than this.

❀

So tell me, friend, who taught the dog so fond before
To turn away his face once he had got it in ?

❦

Her forefeet rest upon the bank, her hind legs ripple in the river
The she-frog heaves on her reflection, as women move above their men.

❀

Cold in the winter he wanders homeless in the snow
Soon though he sweats when warmed by thinking of his wife.

—*Hala*

❧ *From the collection of 700 wittily elegant verses attributed to Hala (c. 500 AD)* ❧

जे मायरं च पियरं च विप्पजहाय पुव्वसंजोगं ।
एगे सहिए चरिस्सामि आरतमेहुणो विवित्तेसी ॥
सुहुमेणं तं परक्कम्म छण्णपएण इत्थीओ मंदा ।
'उवायं पि ताओ जाणंति' जह लिस्संति भिक्खुणो एगे ॥
पासे भिसं णिसीयंति अभिक्खणं पोसवत्थं परिहिंति ।
कायं अहे वि दंसंति 'बाहु मुद्धट्टु कक्खमणुव्वजे' ॥
सयणासणेहिं जोग्गेहिं इत्थीओ एगया णिमंतेंति ।
एयाणि चेव से जाणे पासाणि विरूवरूवाणि ॥
णो तासु चक्खु संधेज्जा णो वि य 'साहसं समणुजाणे' ।
णो सद्धियं पि विहरेज्जा एवमप्पा 'सुरक्खिओ होइ' ॥
कुव्वंति 'पावगं कम्मं' पुट्ठा वेगेवमाहंसु ।
णा हं करेमि पावं ति अंकेसाइणी ममेस त्ति ॥
बालस्स मंदयं बीयं जं च कडं अवजाणई भुज्जो ।
दुगुणं करेइ से पावं पूयणकामो विसण्णेसी ॥
संलोकणिज्जमणगारं आयगयं णिमंतणेणाहंसु ।
वत्थं वा ताइ ! पायं वा अण्णं पाणगं पडिग्गाहे ॥
णीवारमेवं बुज्झेज्जा णो 'इच्छे अगारमागंतुं' ।
'बद्धे विसयपासेहिं' मोहमावज्जइ पुणो मंदे ॥

PRAKRIT

The tempted and the tempting

A monk may leave his former family and kin
Resolved to live alone and partnerless.

But women make their sweet and soft approach
And seek to overcome a monk's defence.

They sit beside him wearing festive clothes
Which part to let him glimpse their bodies' charms.

Or sometimes they will offer him a couch
Which he should recognize as just a trap.

On women such as these his eyes should not be fixed
Nor should he walk with them, but save himself.

Caught in the act of sin, some monks will say :
'There's nothing wrong, she's sleeping in my lap !'

By hypocritically denying it
The fool thus stupidly compounds his sin.

When women call, to tempt a handsome monk :
'Accept this robe, this bowl, sir, and this food !'

'Wild rice to catch a pig !' should be his thought
Turning him from their homes and sensual snares.

—*'Suyagado'*

❧ *A merry excerpt from the ascetic scriptures of the Jains* ❧

तरुणिहि कंत पमुक्किय णिय केलीहरिहि,
सिम्मिर भइण किउ जलणु मरणु अग्गीहरिहि ।
उवभुंजहि केलीरसु अब्भिंतर भुयण,
उज्जाणह दुम्मिहिवि ण कीरइ किवि सयण ॥

मज्जमुक्क संठविउ विरह गंधक्करसु,
पिज्जइ अद्धावट्टउ रसियहि इक्खरसु ।

कुंदचउत्थि वरत्थणि पीणुन्नयथणिय,
णियसत्थरि पलुटंति केवि सीमंतिणिय ॥
केवि दिंति रिउणाहह उपत्तिहि दिणिहि,
णियवल्लह कर केलि लंति सिज्जासणिहि ।
इत्थंतरि पुण पहिय ! सिज्ज इक्कल्लियइ,
पिउ पेसिउ मण दूअउ पिम्म गहिल्लियइ ॥
मइ जाणिउ पिउ आणि मज्झ संतोसिहइ,
णहु मुणिअउ खलु धिट्ठ सोवि महु मिल्हिहइ ।
पिउ णाविउ इहु दूउ गहिवि तत्थवि रहिउ,
सव्व हियउ महु दुक्खि भरिउ पूरिउ अहिउ ॥
णट्ठ मूलु पिअसंगि लाहु इच्छंतियइ ।
णिसुणि पहिय ! जं पढिउ वत्थु विलवंतियइ ॥
मइ घणु दुक्खु सहप्पि मुणवि मणु पेसिउ दूअउ,
णाहु ण आणिउ तेण सुपुणु तत्थव रय हूअउ ।
एम भमंतह सुन्नहियय जं रयणि विहाणिय,
अणिरइ कीयइ कम्मि अवसु मणि पच्छुत्ताणिय ।

मइ दिन्नु हियउ णहु पत्तु पिउ हुई उवम इहु कहु कवण,
सिंगत्थि गइय वाडऽवणी पिक्ख हराविय णिअसवण ॥

APABHRAMSHA

Sadness in springtime

The chill of winter's dying days
Brought girls to huddle round the fire
The sports of love took place indoors
None slept beneath the garden trees.

The wine was laid aside as people drank
Sweet perfumed juices pressed from sugarcane
And heavy-breasted ladies played in bed
To mark the Kundachauthi feast of spring.

In token of the springtime some gave alms
While other women gave their men delight
I lay there lonely longing for my love
And sent my heart to him as messenger.

I thought it would induce my love's return
Quite unaware it would betray my hopes
He kept my treacherous messenger and stayed
So I was burdened with this extra grief.

My capital was lost in hope of gain
Hear now this verse I sorrowfully composed :

> In pain I sent my heart to him
> But there with him it stayed
> Distractedly I spent the night
> Repenting what I'd done
> My heart was gone, I had no man—
> I'll tell you how it was :
> The donkey went in search of horns
> But lost her ears instead.

—*Abd Rahman : 'Sandesharasaka'*

❧ *From a sophisticated treatment of the 'seasons of love' by a 13th century Muslim poet* ❧

چه بلاست از دو چشمت نظرِ نیاز کردن
مژه را کشاد دادن، درِ فتنه باز کردن

چو کمالِ صنعِ بے‌چون ز جمالِ تست پیدا
نتوان حدیثِ عشقت ز رهِ مَجاز کردن

همه خوابِ مردمان شد به دو دیده تلخ، یارب
ز کجات گشت شیرین حرَکاتِ ناز کردن

چه خوش است بادِ خلوت که دهد سرشکِ خونین
ز خراشِ دل گواهی به زبانِ راز کردن

تو بخسپ خوش که مارا ز غمش چو شمع خو شد
همه روز زنده بودن، همه شب گداز کردن

به جفات دل نهادم، بکُن آنچه می توانی
چه کُنم نمی توانم ز تو احتراز کردن

به‌هوس فدا کُنم جان به درت که نیست عارے
پسرِ سبکتگین را هوسِ ایاز کردن

صفِ عاشقانْست اینجا، مده، اے فقیه، زحمت
که به شهرِ بت‌پرستان نتوان نماز کردن

چه بوَد متاعِ خسرو که کُند نثارِ جانان
مگسے چه طعمه رانَد به دهانِ باز کردن؟

Do what you will

Your eyes both cast spellbinding looks
Their opened lids unlock confusion's gates.

Your beauty's form was shaped by God Himself
So are my feelings merely human love ?

Everybody's peace is quite destroyed
Where did you learn this great behaviour from ?

Alone with you, how sweet our silence seems
My bloody tears report my heart's distress.

Sleep soundly then, but I am made by pain
A candle safe by day who melts at night.

Do what you will to me for I'm so used
To cruelty I will not turn aside.

My love's so great I'll offer you my life
Like King Mahmud who loved his slave Ayaz.

These lovers congregate before their idol
So let us have no talk of saying prayers.

What do I have to lay before my love ?
What can the fly know of the falcon's food ?

—*Amir Khusrau*

❧ *A 'ghazal' by Amir Khusrau (d. 1325), the greatest of all the many Persian poets of medieval India* ❧

سرمد غم عشق، بوالهوس را ندهند
سوزِ دل پروانه، مگس را ندهند
عمرے باید، کہ یار آید بہ کنار
این دولت سرمد، همه کس را ندهند

در مسلخِ عشق، جز نکو را نکشند
لاغر صفتان و، زشت خو را نکشند
تو عاشقِ صادقی، ز کشتن مگریز
مردار بود هر آنکه او را نکشند

خواهم، دل پژمرده شود تازه چو گل
جان نغمه سرا بود، به رنگِ بلبل
ایام خزان، بجوشِ بهاری بزنم
با لاله رخے نوش کنم ساغرِ مل

آشفتهٔ آن زلف، گره گیر شدم
تدبیر نه این بود، ز تقدیر شدم
در حلقهٔ آن زلف اسیرم کردند
از شوخیِ عقل، پا به زنجیر شدم

اے لاله رخے، سرو قدے، سیمین تن
ایام بهار است، بکن سیر چمن
چون غنچه مکن حجله نشینی، ستم است
گل میرود و سنبل و نسرین، بوطن

PERSIAN

True lovers have already died

The lustful do not know the aim of love
Do flies know how the moth is set on fire ?
The fullness of true love takes long to learn
In this not everyone has Sarmad's luck.

❦

Love's abattoir is kept to kill the best
Rejecting thin and ugly specimens
By death then be not overawed for if
Your love is true you are already dead.

❀

Can faded heart now freshen like a rose ?
Can this my soul sing like a nightingale ?
This autumn makes me yearn to bring back spring
To drink with him and see his red-flushed cheeks.

❦

I'm maddened by that curling hair
No plan of mine, this must be fate
Those locks have trapped me in their net
My lack of sense has shackled me.

❀

Your tulip face and cypress figure should
Come out into the garden now it's spring
Why tease indoors like some unopened bud
When here the rose and jasmine bloom to fade ?

—*Sarmad*

❧ *The wild Sufism of Sarmad, notorious for loving a Brahmin boy, led to his execution in 1660* ❧

بتے از شوخیِ آهو سرشته نمک پروردهٔ حسن برشته
ادای او هزاران جلوه بردوش نگاه او رمِ آهو در آغوش
نشست و بزم را رشکِ چمن کرد چمن را اخگرے در پیرهن کرد
ندانم دیده ام در عینِ مستی رخش یا قبلهٔ آتش پرستی
نظرها با حیا در گرم جوشی اداها با جفا در خود فروشی
تبسم هائے پنهانی که دانی نمک پاشنده بر زخمِ نهانی
ز هر سو محشرِ نظاره در جوش قیامت حرفے از خاطر فراموش
چو رنگیں جلوهٔ او مجلس آراست ز دلها بے خود ایں هنگام برخاست
چه می باید نشست اے شعلهٔ پرجوش برنگِ آتشِ یاقوت خاموش
شنید ایں نغمه چوں آں شوخِ پرمست بسانِ شعله تند و تیز برجست
چو رقص از شعلهٔ انگیز سر شد ز بادِ دامنِ خود تیزتر شد
به رقصش گرمِ شوخی ها بر و دوش همه اعضا چو موجِ باده در جوش

دلِ عشاق شد در بے قراری ز پایش فتنه ها را دست یاری
نشستن صد بیاباں رم در آغوش ستادن با قیامت دوش بردوش
گهے چوں برق جستن ساز دادے گهے چوں شاخِ گل کج ایستادے
چو بردے بر کمر دست آں اداست شدے موئے کمر خطِ کفِ دست
چو می کردے بدست افشانی انگیز زدے سیلی بروئے زهد و پرهیز
به پاکوبی چو جستے مست از جا شکستے دانهٔ انگورِ دلها
بر دل می آمد از هر دانه آبے ندانم خونِ نابے یا شرابے

The dancing-boy

The lovely boy was light as a gazelle,
Surpassing in his grace and charm. His glance
On entry won the company and set all hearts
On fire. What did they glimpse in ecstasy—
Bright light or what fire-worshippers adore ?
His bashful looks inflamed them, while with cruel
Gestures he roused them to destroy themselves.
You'd think his secret smiles were salt rubbed on
Their hidden wounds. On every side arose
A tumult such as to remove all thought
Of Doomsday's dreadful outcry. When he came
Towards the end of his display, all hearts
Called out : 'O glorious flame, must you die down ?'
Their cry made the seductive charmer, high
Already from his act, spring up again
More fiercely still to blaze and further fan
The flames with draughts made by his spinning robes.
His dance was hot with sensuality as if
His every limb was drunk with wine. His steps
Robbed his admirers' hearts of peace as they
Watched on engrossed as now he rose, now sat,
Now flashed like shafts of lightning, then became
Quite still and drooped to imitate a rose,
His waist still thinner than the lines upon
A lover's hand which sought to clasp it, while
His own hand's movements overwhelmed them all.
His steps crushed all their hearts like grapes
Extracting blood from them—or was it wine ?

—*Ghanimat : 'Nairang-e Ishq'*

❧ *Ghanimat's poem (1685) is one of the few Indian romances with an explicitly gay theme* ❧

Piriti nābhāge piriti nichige
Piriti nājāy ai pari
jimāne khuwābā simāne mere khāba
Piriti premare jari.

❧

Tai je kaliyā aliyā baliyā
Moke kari gali bāul
Jāli katā beredi suhuri mārili
Howā bhātak karili cāul.

❧

Chāge belbelāy kowāi kelkeli kelkelāy
Kāk petar kathā kam
Ene mane lāge tomak ai mainā
Sarirat sumuwāi lam.

❧

Baliyā halo mai aliyā halo mai
Karāke ghurāi ghurāi karo
Ore rātito topani nadhare
Dhāri pātite bāgari phuro.

❧

Bhāto nekhāo mai pānio nekhāo mai
Thāko dhāri pātit sui
Cakuwe cābake nelāge
Sarirat lāgiche jui.

ASSAMESE

The more I want you

Love does not break or snap
Love never drops away
The more you twist love's thread
The tighter grow its coils.

❀

My crazy dark delight
Truly you drive me wild
You whistle through the wall
The rice unboils itself.

❧

The goats bleat and crows caw
But who can my heart tell ?
O how I feel, my love,
Like taking you in me !

❀

I've gone completely wild
Again and again I come
I get no sleep at all
But roll upon my mat.

❧

I want no food or drink
I lie upon my mat
No need to look at him
My body is on fire.

—*Women's folksongs*

❧ *Recorded in the Roman script, these raunchy songs accompany the Bihu dance* ❧

سَمّوڑۓ زین پلپلاں یکے
سَمّوڑۓ درخشکانی براں یکے
سَمّویہ شیشہ ئےشُراوانی
سَمّویہ سردانے تلارانی
سَمّویہ سُہرپُلّے انارانی
سَمّویہ ڈیوائےتہارانی
یاجڑی بُوٹی ئےرغامانی
سَمّویہ ہنجیرمزن تاخیں
کوہ سروکمبائی ترڑۓ رُستہ
ھَندے ماں جیہنیں گراں بیتہ

سرتھٹی ہیچ گواُشۓ نہ چھنڈنیشہ
بُرزۓ کھنت ہونی تکغیں چھمّاں
شف گروخی گوں لاغریں شینکاں
ململی ڈیل گوں ریشمی جَرّاں
دروشماں داچھوتاںہی نوزاں
چھمے شرآں گوں تھنگویں دیمۓ
بمبوئیں جادگوں بارغیں سرینۓ
تُنداں چھوآمٹر داثغیں تیغۓ

BALUCHI

Sammo

Sammo is a fig-tree on the hill
Sammo is a blossom on the bough
Sammo is a flagon of good wine
Sammo is a mountain-bred gazelle
Sammo is a pomegranate flower
Sammo is a lamp bright in the dark
Or a plant the rain's helped grow
Sammo is a fig-tree with broad leaves
On a hill or near a lake
Set in deep-sunk mountain glens
Which no wind can ever shake.

The glances from the red-streaked eye
Are lightning darting from the clouds
Her graceful form in silken clothes
Moves like a cloud from far-off lands
Her face is gold, her eyes are fair
Her hair down to her slender waist
Cuts like a sword-blade, fierce and sharp.

—*Mast Tavakkuli*

❧ *The Marri tribesman Mast Tavakkuli (d. 1885) was driven insane by his impossible love for the married Sammo* ❧

আধক আধ- আধ দিঠি-অঞ্চলে
যব ধরি পেখলুঁ কান।
কত শত কোটি কুসুম-শরে জর জর
রহত কি যাত পরাণ ॥
সজনি, জানলুঁ বিহি মোহে বাম।
দুহুঁ লোচন ভরি যো হরি হেরই
তছু পায়ে মঝু পরণাম ॥ধ্রু॥
সুনয়নি কহত কানু ঘন শ্যামর
মোহে বিজুরি সম লাগি।
রসবতি তাক পরশ-রসে ভাসত
হামারি হৃদয়ে জলু আগি ॥
প্রেমবতি প্রেম লাগি জিউ তেজত
চপল জিবনে মঝু সাধ ।
গোবিন্দদাস ভণে শ্রীবল্লভ জানে
রসবতি-রস-মরিযাদ ॥

BENGALI

Only a lover will know

Only a lover will know how I feel.

The talk all around me is nothing to me
My heart dwells on no one but him.

I work in the house where I have to keep quiet
My love must remain unrevealed.

Alone in my fear like the wife of a thief
I've no one to comfort my heart.

The senior family members all give
Me curses from morning till night.

I suffer because of the one that I love
Unsupported by anyone here.

Here nobody knows the sharp pain in my heart
To whom can I make my complaint ?

So listen to Chandidas : Happiness lies
In letting your love be proclaimed.

—*Chandidas*

❧ *Chandidas (c. 1500) uses motifs from Bengali folksong to express a profound spiritual message* ❧

पीयवा चलेला परदेस, सरब सुख ले ले गयो ।
छतिया पर बजर -केवाड़; ताला कुञ्जी भरि के गयो ॥
तेल फुलेला न लगाइबि; लट छटकाइबि ।
हम ऐसी धनिया अभागिनि; अकेली छोड़ी गयो ॥
गंगा यमुन बीच रेतवा; तेकर बीच बाग लगी ।
ताहि तर सुनरी भइली ठाढ़, नयन दुनो नीर ढरी ॥
घोड़वा चड़ल एक चेलिक ; काहे सुनरी नीर ढरी ।
केकर जोहेलु बाट; नयन दुनो नीर ढरी ॥
तोहरे अइसन पातर पियवा हो; परदेसे गयो ।
उनकेरे जोहिले बाट; नयन दुनो नीर ढरी ॥
लेहु ना सुनरी डाल भरि सोनवा, मोती माँग भरी ।
छोड़ि देहु अइसन बउराह ; लगहु मोरा साथे हरी ॥
आगी लगइबों तोरा डाल भरि सोना; मोती जरि जाहु ।
लवटीहें उहे बउराह, लुटइबों तोरी बरधी धनी ॥

BHOJPURI

The faithful wife

'My love has gone away and taken all my joy
With shutters round his heart locked firmly with a key.

I'll let my hair hang lank with no shampoo or scent
I'm so unfortunate, he's left me here alone.'

Besides the Ganges sands there is a garden laid
And there the woman stands with tears in both her eyes.

A youth rides up to her and asks her why she weeps
And who she's watching for with tears in both her eyes.

'My husband's slim like you but he has gone away
It's him I'm watching for with tears in both my eyes.'

'Oh, take this dish of gold and pearls to dress your hair
Give up that crazy fool and come and be with me.'

'I'll burn your pearls and throw your gold into the fire
My crazy fool will come and take all that you have.'

—*Folksong*

❧ *A beautiful vignette from the rich folk literature of Bhojpuri, situated between Hindi and Bengali* ❧

Dalayaō bananoi dikhar nanga nanga
Daōalay mano gabdong
Habab dukharu nongboco ang baydi
Gōcōni daha nama ?

Daōno hōrdonghay zonomaō zuli
Agno hōrdong hay dahalō khali
Cimangaō nongkhōu nupherbayo
Mokhthngaō gomor lango.

❦

Bar ciu ciu bardong
Gaōlang gaōdang bibara hōnoi bardong
Cikhiria bahang birhang bidoi cobdong
Habap inoino modom phoidong.

Bōngphangaō bananoi Lapha caikhō dawa gabdon
Roicumoi moicumoi cōnde bōnde ringlangdong
Ayō habab ma ece mozang din zadong.

❧

Biliphang phōrōraō lapha caykhō daōwa
Hadaōri bidaōri mano gapdon ?
Bini gap nayaō angni bikhaya
Alōuhap khalōuhap mano zadong !

Bikhani dahakhōu bikha thalayaō donnanoi
Zuzayni ōrgengaō mon mon khamza nanoi
Zabay dong coi habap ayō anglay
Goconi gap nayaō phothong nathong.

BODO

The songs of the birds

What is that mournful song
The bird sings on the tree ?
Is your heart heavy too ?
Are you as sad as me ?

The bird will find its mate
But I must suffer pain
I see you in my dreams
You're gone when I awake.

❦

The breezes gently blow
The blossom is in bloom
The dancing butterfly
Sucks nectar from the flowers.

These sweet perfumes, this shining sun
These birdsongs fill the countryside
This day seems made for love.

❧

The night has just arrived
A bird begins to sing
Her plaintive song reflects
The pain of being apart.

Within my heart I feel
Sad echoes of her song
I too lie here apart
Quite helpless and quite lost.

—*Three folksongs*

❧ *The natural imagery of these tribal folksongs from Assam is wonderfully fresh* ❧

Kḥank nā larzīrah lakas qarzīrah
Dandānk sadafnā buřzī lawangnā
Kḥankū kḥařanā tambū nařanā
Gūdī gidān nā pullus urānā
Purkā kḥawāhī dīr nā dawā hī
Gūdī shakar kḥor natte buřzā tor !

Tūtanā ṭāřī pūskunā yārī
Shāmaṭ shānūzān jwānītī janūzān
Mullānā bānghī Souzūnā sāngī
^{c}Atarus ^{c}atras kāṭum nā chatrus
Jamḍāk janḍītā zulfāk ranḍītā
Dānge arāngē sangī barāmī
Gūdī pullā kḥor bālā dī shar tor !

Kḥwāja gūdī ko kḥidmatta tē mūri ko
Bāragi hurbo kasarāi salīsunī
Sūzūhī hurbo ^{c}ishqati bāsunī
Dostus dostus kani hazār dostus
Dosti ṭahpak nītū ai be bāmus
Nālat ki maruī hand'nā be bakḥti
Khoṭi kuntū handū elū tū neki !

Brahui

Why did she marry another ?

Your eyes are magic worth a *lakh* of rupees
Your early teeth are tall as cinnamon trees
Your ram-like eyes are pleasant as a tent
You're mistress of the camp, the home's best flower
The water that you bring is elixir
Go on, my sweet-toothed love, lift up your feet !

My mulberry branch, you have another man
You light up evening, widowed in your youth
The priest proclaims that Souzu is betrothed
Your head's a sunshade, you are all perfume
Your hair-do and jewellery are just like a whore's
First she is betrothed and next she's married
My *pulao*-loving darling, up you go !

Now see how Barag stands upon the road
Now see how Souzu is eaten up with love
You are my dear, my dear, my dearest one
But no, you're shamelesss, dear to me no more
I'm so unlucky, I'm mocked by everyone
To me she's false, to another she is true !

—*Anonymous*

❧ *'The one Brahui song fit for civilized ears' which a rueful missionary collector of 1881 could find* ❧

ठंडा पानी चिट्टी चाननी रातीं श्रोल्ले पतलू दा नाड़ा
पानी पीना तेरे हत्थें दा गोरिये !
लेश्रां तूं लोटे गी मांजी !

लोकें दे बागें फुलनूं जे फुल्लेंदे,
माहड़े जो बागें केले,
श्रज्जै दी रातीं मिलना तां मिली लै
फिरी संजोगां दे मेले !

लोकें दे बागें फुलनूं जे फुल्ले दे,
माहड़े जो बागें गोबी,
लैने देने दी गल्ल नि गोरिये
नैनां तेरेश्रां दा लोभी ।।

श्रो किल्लिया बत्तना छोड़ी दित्ता
इब्बै साथें साथें भरी ल्यौन्नियां पानी
श्रो किल्लिया बत्तना छोड़ी दित्ता !

बुरा बो लोग इस गंगथा दा
श्रनदोसियेंगी दोस दिन्दा ऐ जानी
श्रो किल्लिया बत्तना छोड़ी दित्ता !

कियाँ कुसै कन्ने हस्सना बोलना ?
कियाँ कुसै कन्ने गल्ल गलानी ?
श्रो किल्लिया बत्तना छोड़ी दित्ता !

सिक्ख देश्रां मिकी देवी दित्तेश्रा,
कियाँ में सस्स ननान मनानी ?
श्रो किल्लिया बत्तना छोड़ी दित्ता !

DOGRI

Keeping the pitcher clean

Cool water flows beneath the moon
I'll drink to you, my beauty
So keep your pitcher clean for me.

In other gardens flowers bloom
Bananas grow in mine
If we're to meet, let's meet tonight
Let's not leave things to future chance.

In other gardens flowers bloom
But cabbages in mine
I will not wheel and deal, my beauty
You are my eyes' one true desire.

❦

No more will I go to the well by myself
I fetch water along with the rest of the girls
No more will I go to the well by myself.

The villagers here are all cruel and unkind
Although they accuse me I have done no wrong
No more will I go to the well by myself.

How can anyone laugh ? How can anyone talk ?
How can anyone speak to anyone here ?
No more will I go to the well by myself.

My mother-in-law and my sister-in-law
Are always suspecting me—what can I do ?

No more will I go to the well by myself.

—*Two songs*

Dogri is the language of the Jammu hills to the south of Kashmir

(अह) नयण-कडक्खिहिँ आहणए वांकउ जोवंती
ह्राव-भाव-सिगार-भंगि नव-नविय करंति ॥
तह वि न भीजइ मुणि-पवरोँ तउ वेस बोलावइ
'तवण तुल्लु तुह विरह, नाह! मह तणु संतावइ ॥

बारहँ वरिसहँ तणउ नेहु किणि कारणि छंडिउ
एवडु निट्ठुरमणउँ काइँ मू-सिँउ तुँम्हि मंडिउ ॥
थूलिभद्द पभणेइ 'वेस! अइ-खेदु न कीजइ
लोहिहि घडियउ हियउ मज्झ, तुह वयणि न भीजइ' ॥

'मह विलवंतिय-उवरि, नाह! अणुराग धरीजइ
एरिसु पावस-कालु सयलु मू-सिँउ माणीजइ' ॥
मुणिवइ जंपइ 'वेस! सिद्धि-रमणी परिणेवा
मणु लीणउ संजम-सिरीहिँ सिउँ भोग रमेवा' ॥

भणइ कोस 'साचउँ कियउँ "नवलइ राचइ लोउ।
मू मिल्हिवि संजम-सिरिहिँ जउ रातउ मुणि-राउ' ॥

HINDI

Love is sovereign

Do not speak ill of love, for love is sovereign
The body with no love is deadlier than the grave.

❦

The play of love upon the body's vein-stringed lute
Is heard by none besides the Lord or else the soul.

❧

I make my life a wick to light my body's lamp
With fuel from my blood : when shall I see his face ?

❀

These tears of mine are friends which keep the world at bay
The eye that flows with blood is witness to true love.

❦

I wander through the hills with eyes worn out by tears
I cannot find the herb of everlasting life.

❧

My eyes are burnt with tears, yet still I search for you
You do not come, I suffer—that is my complaint.

❀

The heart may be on fire but who can see the smoke ?
We know, though, if we burn—the arsonist knows too !

—*Kabir*

❧ *Kabir (15th century) is the greatest of the many low-caste saint-poets of medieval India* ❧

पेम सुनत मन भूल न राजा। कठिन पेम, सिर देइ तौ छाजा॥
पेम-फाँद जो परा न छूटा। जीउ दीन्ह पै फाँद न टूटा॥
गिरगिट छंद धरै दुख तेता। खन खन पीत, रात, खन सेता॥
जान पुछार जो भा बनबासी। रोंव रोंव परे फँद नगवासी॥
पाँखन्ह फिरि फिरि परा सो फाँदू। उड़ि न सकै, अरुझा भा बाँदू॥
'मुयों मुयों' अहनिसि चिल्लाई। ओही रोस नागन्ह धै खाई॥
पंडुक, सुआ, कंक वह चीन्हा। जेहिं गिउ परा चाहि जिउ दीन्हा॥
तितिर-गिउ जो फाँद है, निति पुकारै दोख।
सो कित हँकार फाँद गिउ (मेलै) कित मारे होइ मोख॥
राजै लीन्ह ऊबि कै साँसा। ऐस बोल जिनि बोलु निरासा॥
भलेहि पेम है कठिन दुहेला। दुइ जग तरा पेम जेइ खेला॥
दुख भीतर जो पेम-मधु राखा। जग नहिं मरन सहै जो चाखा॥
जो नहिं सीस पेम-पथ लावा। सो प्रिथिमी महँ काहे क आवा?॥
अब मैं पंथ पेम सिर मेला। पाँव न ठेलु, राखु कै चेला॥
पेम-बार सो कहै जो देखा। जो न देख का जान विसेखा?॥
तौ लगि दुख पीतम नहिं भेंटा। मिलै, तौ जाइ जनम-दुख मेटा॥
जस अनूप, तू बरनेसि, नखसिख बरनु सिंगार।
है मोहिं आस मिलै कै, जौ मेरवै करतार॥

Hindi (Avadhi)

Love's noose marks all

Be sure, O king, that love is hard and paid for with one's life
There is no slipping from its noose, which even death breaks not
Its pains shift like the chameleon's shades, from yellow, red to white
The snaking marks of love's lasso are on the peacock's tail
By ever filling on his wings they stop him flying high
In rage he mews 'I'm dead, I'm dead,' and eats the jungle snakes
That deadly noose rings many throats : the parrot's, dove's and kite's
So marked, the partridge cries in guilt and hopes
To draw the hunter's hand to set him free.

With heavy sigh, the king replied : Enough of this despair !
Love may be hard but must be played, to pass through life to heaven
It is honey in a box of pain, whose taste will set us free
Why come into this world unless to give up all for love ?
My head is laid upon love's path, so teach me now its ways
For he alone can tell of love who has been inside its gate
Till lovers meet they suffer pain, once met all pain is lost
Since you have seen her now describe the looks
From head to foot of her whom I desire to meet.

—*Muhammad Jayasi : 'Padmavat'*

From a Sufi romance of 1540, in which the royal hero gets advice from the heroine's parrot

बैठी मानिनी गहि मौन ।
मनौ सिद्ध समाधि सेवत सुरनि साधे पौन ॥
अचल आसन, पलक तारी, गुफा घूँघट-भौन ।
रोषही कौ ध्यान धारे टेक टारै कौन ॥
अबहिं जाइ मनाइ लीजै, अवसि कीजै गौन ।
सूर के प्रभु जाइ देखौ, चित्त चौंधी जौन ॥

यह ऋतु रूसिबे की नाहीं ।
बरषत मेघ मेदिनी कैं हित, प्रीतम हरषि मिलाहीं ॥
जेती बेलि ग्रीष्म ऋतु डाहीं, ते तरवर लपटाहीं ।
जे जल बिनु सरिता ते पूरन, मिलन समुद्रहिं जाहीं ॥
जोबन धन है दिवस चारि कौ, ज्यौं बदरी की छाहीं ।
मैं दंपति-रस-रीति कही है, समुझि चतुर मन माहीं ॥
यह चित धरि री सखी राधिका, दै दूती कौं बाहीं ।
सूरदास उठि चली री प्यारी, मेरैं सँग पिय पाहीं ॥

HINDI (BRAJ BHASHA)

Radha's jealous rage with Krishna

She proudly sits in silence
In trance as if from yogic breath control.

Immobile, eyelids closed, with covered head
But who'll endure the rage she meditates ?

'Now go and calm her,' Radha's friend tells Krishna
'Go and you'll see how furious she is.'

❦

'This is no time for anger
The rains are falling, lovers are united.

The heat-burnt creepers clasp the trees afresh
Once dried-up rivers flow down to the sea.

Youth is soon gone, a passing cloud-cast shadow—
I've told you so much else of partnership.

Be sensible and come,' says Radha's friend.
'Come then to *your* dear Krishna,' she replies.

—Surdas

❧ *Two songs on the love of Radha and Krishna by the still immensely popular poet Surdas (c. 1500)* ❧

डीठिबरत बाँधी अटनु, चढ़ि धावत न डरात ।
इतहिँ उतहिँ चित दुहुनु के नट लौँ आवत जात ॥

अँगुरिनु उचि, भरु भीति दै, उलमि चितै चख लोल ।
रुचि सौँ दुहूँ दुहूँनु के चूमे चारु कपोल ॥

झटकि चढ़ति उतरति अटा, नैँक न थाकति देह ।
भई रहति नट कौ बटा अटकी नागर-नेह ॥

उड़ति गुड़ी लखि ललन की अँगना अँगना माँह ।
बौरी लौँ दौरी फिरति छुवति छबीली छाँह ॥

ऊँचैँ चितै सराहियतु गिरह कबूतरु लेतु ।
झलकित दृग, मुलकित बदनु, तनु पुलकित किहिँ हेतु ॥

छिनकु चलति, ठठुकति छिनकु, भुज प्रीतम-गल-डारि ।
चढ़ी अटा देखति घटा बिज्जु-छटा सी नारि ॥

चाह भरीँ, अति रस भरीँ, बिरह भरीँ सब बात ।
कोरि सँदेसे दुहुनु के चले, पौरि लौँ जात ॥

Hindi (Braj Bhasha)

Glimpses

Their glances stretched between the rooftops form
A tightrope for brave lovers' hearts to cross.

❦

First making sure none watches them, they stand on tiptoe
Then lean across the wall between for eager kisses.

❀

Up to the roof she goes to look, then down
Untiring, like a yo-yo on love's string.

❧

Above her yard she sees her lover's kite
And madly runs about to chase its shadow.

❦

You praise those pigeons tumbling in the sky
Who is it though who made you look so thrilled ?

❀

With arm around him, now she moves, then stops
Flashing like lightning on her balcony.

❧

Their hearts so full of love, their talk so full of pain
A million signals sent while walking to the door.

—*Biharilal*

❧ *These elegant Hindi verses by the 17th poet Biharilal are in the tradition of the Prakrit poet Hala* ❧

ಕಂಗಳಲ್ಲಿ ಕಾಂಬೆನೆಂದು
ಕತ್ತಲೆಯ ಹೊಕ್ಕಡೆಂತಹುದಯ್ಯಾ?
ಬೆಟ್ಟದ ತುದಿಯ ಮೆಟ್ಟಲೆಂದು
ಹಳ್ಳಕೊಳ್ಳಂಗಳಲ್ಲಿ ಇಳಿದಡೆಂತಹುದಯ್ಯಾ?
ನೀನಿಕ್ಕಿದ ಸಯಿದಾನವನೊಲ್ಲದೆ
ಬೇರೆ ಬಯಸಿದಡೆಂತಹುದಯ್ಯಾ?
ಚೆನ್ನಮಲ್ಲಿಕಾರ್ಜುನನ ಘನವನರಿಯಲೆಂದು
ಕಿರುಕುಳಕ್ಕೆ ಸಂದಡೆಂತಹುದಯ್ಯಾ?

ಅರಿಸಿನವನೆ ಮಿಂದು ಹೊಂದೊಡಿಗೆಯನೆ ತೊಟ್ಟು
ದೇವಾಂಗವನುಟ್ಟೆ;
ಪುರುಷ ಬಾರಾ
ನಿನ್ನ ಬರವೆನ್ನಸುವಿನ ಬರವು ಬಾರಯ್ಯಾ
ಚೆನ್ನಮಲ್ಲಿಕಾರ್ಜುನಯ್ಯಾ
ನೀನು ಬಂದಹನೆಂದು ಬಟ್ಟೆಯ ನೋಡಿ ಬಾಯಾರುತ್ತಿಹೆನು.

ಹಗಲು ನಾಲ್ಕು ಜಾವ ನಿಮ್ಮ ಕಳವಳದಲ್ಲಿಪ್ಪೆನು.
ಇರುಳು ನಾಲ್ಕು ಜಾವ ನಿಮ್ಮ ವಿಕಳಾವಸ್ಥೆಯಲ್ಲಿಪ್ಪೆನು
ಹಗಲಿರುಳು ನಿಮ್ಮ ಹಂಬಲದಲ್ಲಿ ಮೈಮರೆದೊರಗಿದೆನು
ಚೆನ್ನಮಲ್ಲಿಕಾರ್ಜುನಯ್ಯ
ನಿಮ್ಮ ಒಲುಮೆ ನಟ್ಟು ಹಸಿವು, ತೃಷೆ, ನಿದ್ರೆಯ ತೊರೆದೆನಯ್ಯಾ

KANNADA

How would it be ?

How will it be if I entered the dark
And hoped I could see with my eyes ?
How would it be if I entered the valley
And hoped I could stand on the peaks ?
How would it be if I turned from Your grace
To allow myself other desires ?
How would it be if I looked in those base ones
For Lord Mallikarjuna's glory ?

❀

'I have bathed in turmeric and dressed
In cloth of gold and silken gown—
O come, my Lord ! My husband, come !
Your advent grants me life afresh !'
My mouth is dry from crying out
I wait for Mallikarjuna to come.

❦

I long for You the whole day long
I pine for you throughout the night
Oblivious of myself I yearn, my Lord
My love for Mallikarjuna makes me
Forget my hunger, thirst and sleep.

—*Akka Mahadevi*

❧ *'Vacana' verses written in the 13th century by a Bhakti yogini in praise of her Lord Cenna Mallikarjuna, or Shiva* ❧

ژیٚ کمیو سوٚنہٕ میانہٕ برٛم دِتھہٕ نیوٗنکھو
ژیٚ کیہو زِہ گیُی میانٕی دٕی
ژکھ ترٛاو دٕی ٹالہِ دٕ دٕ بنٕدہٕ چھوٗی نا اِوان
ژیٚ کیہو زِہ گیُی میانٕی دٕی
نیٚصیف راتٕن بر وُتھی ترٛاوٕ میو
ساتھاہ پکِھنا ژٕی
پھیرہ چھنہ کینہہ تہٕ پھیرہ چھکہ پاوان
ژیٚ کیہو زِہ گیُی میانٕی دٕی
شرٛاوٕنیٚن شیٖنس زن بوٚہ گلان آیس
باغس پھوٚجِس بوٚہ ہیٚنی
چوٗنٕی باغ تےٚ ژٕی دوہ لوبھاوان
ژیٚ کیہو زِہ گیُی میانٕی دٕی
اوٚش چھس ترٛاوان بوٚہ ژالہِ ژاسے
میٚہ بالہ گوژ ہم ژٕی
ژہٕ کہٕ دوو وتہٕ میانہٕ آکھ مُشراوان
ژیٚ کہٕ دوو گیُی میانٕی دٕی

KASHMIRI

My love, why do you hate me now ?

Which rival wife has turned you from me ?
My love, why do you hate me now ?
Please stop this anger and resentment
My love, why do you hate me now ?

At midnight still my door stood open
In case you'd come, however briefly
We two are one, you've made us separate
My love, why do you hate me now ?

I'm melting like the snow in summer
I'm flowering like the garden jasmine
The garden's yours, come in, enjoy it
My love, why do you hate me now ?

I'm shedding floods of bitter tears
For you alone I'm filled with longing
Have you forgotten all about me ?
My love, why do you hate me now ?

—*Habba Khatun*

Habba Khatun (c. 1550) was a village girl who married the last independent ruler of Kashmir

Cung-ḍa' no goḍjhung-te ber rutu peḍ-te
Ber rutu peḍ-te, re ?

Ḍurib belong konsel ḍa' ol-na col-ta
Ṙomoḍ-ḍa' gur-ta, romoḍ-ḍa' gur-ta !

'Dhae^{n} se, re bhai joi, ma^{n}-te gam-goṙ-e-m
Apa-te utun-goṙ-e-m iny um-iny co-na !

Hae iny-a' ma^{n} joi, bhai^{n}si no ob-song-goṙ-e
Kon-tang no ob-song-goṙ-e iny um-iny co-na !'

Ɛ-re e-re merom-gupa-ki, e-re e-re bheři-gupa-ki
Ata senghor, re babu, boini col-ki ?

Kunḍab mugam bheři-gupa-ki,
Han-tij u-tij merom-gupa-ki.
Ata senghor, re babu, boini-na-ing col-ki ?

Kinir jhangkoe biru ga'řha
Kiřo' banae bhore-si'-moe
Ata goḍjhung, re babu, boini-na-ing col-ki ?

Bokob-te khapa-kon
Lutui-te rango'-si'
Iam-ga toro'-ga mu'sing-tij col-ki !

KHARIA

Who's playing the flute ?

On the way to the well who's playing the flute
Who's playing the flute ?

A *durib*-ripe girl is off to the well
O how the tears flow, O how the tears flow !

'Run quickly !' she says to her brother. 'Go tell
Our mother and father I'm not coming back.

Dear mother can sell off the buffalo now
Or sell the calf too, for I'm not coming back !'

❦

'O goatherds and you shepherds say
Which way has my darling gone ?

I've goatherds here and goatherds there
I've shepherds on both sides of me
Which way has my darling gone ?

These jungle-thickets, hills and caves
Hold many tigers, many bears
Which way has my darling gone ?'

'With hands about her head
With clothes that flew about
Weeping and wailing she went east !'

—*Two folksongs*

❧ *The Kharia tribal people of North-Eastern India speak a language of the Munda family* ❧

نکان غمو دا ستانو تہ پردشٹہ اظہار آرتیام
گلائی لاکھ تتے کندوری ہزار آرتیام

نہان ادشتوئی سردیو راز مہ ہمو نیہ پیت
جنیسین بے دس بتیتی تان راز دا ٹکار آرتیام

ترختی ادشوئے مرہا شدا تہ نو بوشی
کندوری عمرد موتزا دا نگاہ ای دیدار آرتیام

صدا قتت بوا رتیام آفرین کورے تو متے
ہر حریفو ہر دیا ہمیشہ ای انگار آرتیام

ہیجی ادشوئے دیران عشقو چمن مہ سار پردشی
حتیتی ھیہ جمنا اجی نوبہار آرتیام

پوشتیام بو پروانان جیر بتیتی انگاروت گیادا
شیرین زرا لو تہ نیچے ھتتان غون بنجار آرتیام

خضا لبت تتے لو بوس شامل مہ یہ جیرا بیکا
کوکی، اجازت مشکتیام نہ تہ سار بنجار آرتیام

صابروت ہوئے نصیب ھنوک خیرتی دیدار عمرا
پوشیکایت خدا یار سلام ہزار بار آرتیام

KHOWAR

Now my love is told

This tale of my grief has been told
And all these complaints have been made.

The pain in my heart which lay hidden
Is a secret I've had to reveal.

How slowly the time passed without you
Till at last I could glimpse you again.

Now praise me for being so true
I've set all my rivals on fire.

New spring have I brought to these gardens
I once left decayed in the fall.

Drawn on like a moth to the flame
My life is made sacrifice to you.

To you no distress did this cause
By me no permission was asked.

If this was the last time we'd meet
I'd say : God be with you, my dear !

—*Sabir*

A modern 'ghazal' in the language of Chitral in Northern Pakistan

Chavei chacha i cha teula
Longdu deupa na cha saikha la ta
Ra pa ta sikhong chine !

Deu cha vana kei ma nai ta
Sei ta ki pa mai haw he ta
Ne chhong kong reu lia i lai zo lo aw !

Na me me cha na pi leu la
Cheu rapa ta song
Ro eu vei e !

A sai pata pa sai vana
Khang khang paw
Cha isang pa aw na !

Cha ta ta kha kei ma long duh
Vasa i cha ngia na lai aw pa ei kha hria cha
A vaw hnang aw ma ?

Na song ro cha, cha lua tua la kaima i cha
Khang khang kawh hra na
Veu hai li hua la hnai va pi e !

LAKHER

The girls sing back to the boys

The boys :

You two lovely sisters on each side of me
I do so love both of you, but I'm afraid
You'll laugh if I say : 'Wait, get married to me !'

The girls :

O never will we marry, O never at all
Instead we will stay here together at home
As close and as tight as two horns on a ram !

❧

The boys :

O let me feel your breasts
I long to marry you
I cannot pay the price !

The girls :

You cannot feel for free
I'm saving myself for
The man who'll marry me !

The boys :

I love you, don't say no
Who will know if I have
One feel to remember by ?

The girls :

I love you too, but first
My parents must be paid
We'll sleep together then !

—*Folksongs*

❧ *Ritualized group songs from the hills of Assam where tribal girls show off their self-confidence* ❧

आकुल चिकुर वेढल मुख–सोभ
राहु कएल ससि–मण्डल–लोभ ॥

उभरल चिकुर माल कर रङ्ग
जनि जमुना-जल गाङ्ग-तरङ्ग ॥

बड अपुरुब दुहु चेतन–मेलि
विपरित रति कामिनि कर केलि ॥

हास–सोहाओन सम–जल–विन्दु
मदन मोति दए पूजल इन्दु ॥

पिआ-मुख सुमुखि चूम्ब तेंजि ओज
चान्द अधोमुख पिबए सरोज ॥

कुच विपरीत विलम्बित हार
कनक-कलश जनि दूधक धार ॥

किङ्किणि रनित नितम्बहि छाज
मदन-महासिधि-बाजन बाज ॥

MAITHILI

The moon looks down

Her hair hangs loosely down and hides her lovely face
As if the planet's node desired the moon's eclipse.

The broken garland on her hair looks wonderful
Like Ganges-waves upon the river Yamuna.

How fine a sight the youthful couple make
What joy the girl has as she lies on top of him.

Her smile shines amidst the droplets of her sweat
It seems that Cupid offers pearls up to the moon.

The fair-faced girl showers kisses on her husband
And seems a moon turned down to suck the lotus up.

The garland hanging over her inverted breasts
Looks like a stream of milk which pours from golden jars.

Her little tinkling bells look so lovely on her hips
Their sound marks Cupid's glorious triumph.

—*Vidyapati*

❧ *The frank eroticism is characteristic of the great 15th century love-poet*

ആരോ മനോഹര സർവ്വാംഗിയാമിവ-
ളാരോമലാൾക്കിത്ര വെമ്പലെന്തോ?
നീളെയുത്തുംഗമാം മാർത്തട്ടലയുന്നു
തോളണിത്തൂവെള്ളച്ചേലയ്ക്കുള്ളിൽ.

കെട്ടഴിഞ്ഞാമനപ്പൃഷ്ഠഭാഗത്തെയും
പൃഷ്ഠനിതംബപ്പരപ്പിനേയും
മൂടിക്കിടക്കുന്നു മുഗ്ദ്ധമാം കാർകുഴൽ
നീടാർന്ന നീലത്തഴയ്ക്കു തുല്യം;
ഇക്കരിരുൾച്ചുരുൾ തൊട്ടഴിയുന്നിതോ
തൃക്കരംകൊണ്ടിരുൾപോക്കും ചന്ദ്രൻ!

ഭവ്യപരിമളമൊന്നിതാ, പൂത്തൊരു
ദിവ്യലതയിൽ നിന്നെന്നപോലെ
സുന്ദരിതങ്കൽനിന്നേററിടചേരുന്നു
ചന്ദനശീതള ചന്ദ്രികയിൽ
ഏകയാണേണാക്ഷി കാമുകസന്നിധി
പൂകുവാൻ പോവുകയായിരിക്കാം;
തൻപള്ളിവാളേന്തി പ്രച്ഛന്നമൂർത്തിയായ്
മുമ്പിൽ നടക്കുന്നുമുണ്ടാം പ്രേമം!
ഉല്ലസിക്കട്ടെ യഥേഷ്ടമായ് മന്മഥൻ!
അല്ല,ഭിസാരികയല്ലിത്തന്വി:
ശങ്കയോ ഭീതിയോ തീണ്ടിയിട്ടില്ലല്ലോ,
തങ്കപ്പൂപോലുള്ള തന്മുഖത്തെ.
അല്ലായ്കിലീയഭിസാരികയ്ക്കാവക
വല്ലായ്മകൾക്കില്ല ബന്ധമൊന്നും:
ഏവരുമാരെയഭിസരിക്കേണം,മാ-
ദ്ദേവനെത്തേടിക്കിപ്പോളിവൾ.

MALAYALAM

Approaching the Lord

But who is this approaching now in fear
So lovely yet so filled with nervousness ?
Her snow-white robe slips from her shoulders so
It barely hides her softly heaving breast.

In dark cascades her lustrous tresses glide
Down the length of her proudly-arching back
At last to coil around her shapely hips
And while the moon is known to have the power
To pierce all normal dark with light, yet here
It crowns those tresses' darkness with its rays.

And as she hurries onward through the night
The passing of her beauty emanates
Perfumes as heady as a jasmine-bloom
To blend with the cool sandal-scented moon.

She goes alone. Perhaps her footsteps take
Her to a lovers' meeting-place, perhaps
Great Kamaveda, god of love, although
Invisible, precedes her to prepare
Love's charming rout—but no, this cannot be
Some girl infatuated with a man.
No fears or doubts inhabit this fair face
For to desire she is a stranger now
She seeks none but that Boundless Lord in whom
All men must find their final trysting-place.
Here sufferers find the balm for all their woes—
Can hearts reach any higher bliss than this ?

—Vallattol : 'Magdalana Mariyam'

❧ Mary Magdalene's loving approach to Jesus is evoked by a 20th century Hindu poet from Kerala, Christianity's oldest home in India ❧

आधिल्या भ्रतारें काम नव्हे पुरा । ह्मणोनि व्यभिचारा टेकलियें ॥
रात्रंदिस मज पाहिजे जवळी । क्षण त्यानिराळी न गमे घडी ॥
नाम गोष्टी माझी सोय सांडा आतां । रातलें अनंता तुका ह्मणे ॥

वाळो जन मज ह्मणोत शिंदळी । परि हा वनमाळी न विसंबें ॥
सांडूनि लौकिक जालियें उदास । नाहीं भय आस जीवित्वाची ॥
नाइकें वचन बोलतां या लोकां । ह्मणे जालों तुका हरिरता ॥

अइकाल परी ऐसें नव्हे बाई । न संडा या सोई भ्रताराची ॥
नव्हे आराणुक लौकिकापासून । आपुल्या आपण गोविलें तें ॥
तुका म्हणे मन कराल कठीण । त्या या निवडोन मजपाशी ॥

परपुरुषाचें सुख भोगे तरी । उतरोनि करीं घ्यावें सीस ॥
संवसारा आगी आपुलेनि हातें । लावूनि मागुतें पाहूं नये ॥
तुका म्हणे व्हावें तयापरी धीट । पतंग हा नीट दीपासोई ॥

Just go for it

My husband wasn't up to it—
I'm having this affair
I want my lover night and day
I hate to be apart
So Tuka says : Forgetting all
I have to be with Him !

I'll not forget Him even though
people call me Whore
To live or die's the same to me
past all caring now
So Tuka says : I do not hear them
He's the one I want !

You women listen : Things are not
at all as you have heard
These husbands that you're tied to cannot
give happiness, you know
So Tuka says : Be tough and leave
them all to follow me !

❧

To make the most of an affair
place your head on hand
Set all your normal life on fire
never looking back
So Tuka says : Just go for it
like a moth for flame !

—Tukaram

❧ *The low-caste saint-poet Tukaram (d. 1649) composed 4,000 of these outspoken 'abhang' verses* ❧

Bo tama risa risa
Supid kedam ranga nacha
Nida singi, ba-gem gututana
Nama nagen jige lotana

Andutadam sakomtadam
Hotore do hisir mena
Polatamdo chilka saritana
Nama nagen jige lotana.

❧

Bhati ora piti piri, honortanaking juri juri
Niral sobha nelotanaking, kulgeaking bano hiating
Nawa hiriti piritiking, bano hiating, re-gating

Samrom rupa munga mala, sasang-sari katare pola
Jiure do rajijanaking, bano hiating, re gating
Nawa hiriti piritiking, bano hiating, re gating.

❧

Natagota bano uru, nutanaking puru puru
Jiu redo raji-janaking, banohiating, re-gatim.

MUNDARI

Getting together

I love your head with waving hair
Tied in a bun with scarlet thread
While you keep weaving wreaths of flowers
I long for you with burning heart.

I love the bangles on your wrist
The shining necklace round your neck
The toe-ring jingles on your feet
I long for you with burning heart.

❧

The couple pass the wineshop, arm in arm
With graceful movement, free from saddening thoughts
Their new-found joy casts out all cares and fears.

With yellow clothes and ornaments of gold
With hearts that beat as one, all gloom is gone
When love unites, farewell to cares and fears.

❧

The more they drink the less they think of who is who
Forgetting everything as heart is joined to heart.

—*Three folksongs*

❧ *The life of the 'native Indian' tribespeople is reflected in the colour and intoxication of these songs* ❧

Vichosale pono Mezatso

Lö keghü-lo nyie ke-vi po ba
Kebao-chü sone rho-wa ghe ?
Kebo-chü shiegwulene rho
Tsüo sevâ n nü-o nye thü.

Sü-o sene teva vâ ne whe
Ke-vâ zü a mi-ne po to-lo
Ke-vâ zü we kha meta-wa khü
Kha meta khü khwenü sü mba.

Mba zoba mi ke-ta khwel
Mi ta-ta tswe lo-su-ji ke-po.
O-mi zhü to n thu phwe walo.

❧

Hiewe so mu kebi-mià ze-lo
Nie zhü ri pfü
Nie khrunho keta zolieyalo
A si kemo-u !

NAGA (ANGAMI)

Girls sing to their lovers

Vichosale loves Mezatso . . .

Beside the river grows a flower
Who was it who picked it then ?
It was my love who picked the flower
For me to put behind my ear.

I came with it to you at night
But this made people talk of you
You wouldn't let me go at night
You grabbed my clothes and sat on them.

We sat there till they went away
When all had gone we talked at last
Take off your bracelets, sleep with me !

❧

If I'm not good enough for you
Go find yourself a girl who is—
A girl to take your hoe for you
Your raincoat woven out of leaves
My lover, you are dumb !

—*Two girls' songs*

दिउँसो घाम रातीलाई सूर्य जुन्
कोइ दिनमा संझौली मेरो गुन
तिम्रो हाम्रो भेटभाको दिन
संग्लो पानी धमिलो मन किन ?
घर त मेरो यां हैन दूवाकोट
छोडा नजाउ मालती फूलको बोट
मछुँ मत समाइदेउ घांटी
दया गर्ने को छ र मं माथि
आठाना सेरको खसीको मासु
खूब खायो राँचीमा
कान्छीको माया बहुतै लाग्छ
परेली· आंखीमा
दिउँसो घाम रातीको सूर्य जून
कोइ दिनमा संझौला मेरो गुन ।
हिङ् जीरा खानु, मरीचै खानु सुपारी कुटुक्कै,
फागुनको भाखा, माहुरीको चाका संझनु सुटुक्कै,
माया तिम्लाई संझन्छु छिन्काछिन्
मेरो मन रोइरहन्छ रातो दिन् !
मधेशै ज्यान्को एकदन्ते हात्ती
घाँस खान्छ गोपे बाँस
आफूको मुहार नदेखे सम्म
मन हुन्छ एक तमास्
धानको बाला मकइको जमरा
तिमी फूल म हौंला भंमरा
रानी है वनको चिरूरा दाउरा

NEPALI

I'm good for you

A sun by day, a night-time sun
I'm good for you, remember too
That happy day when first we met
Clear water, why this clouded heart ?
This Nuwakot is not my home
Do not leave, my jasmine flower
I shall die, so hold me tight
Who have I to be kind to me ?
Four pounds of meat for one rupee
In Ranchi what a feast we had !
Her eyes with long rich lashes draw
Me on to love dear youngest sister.

A sun by day, a night-time sun
I'm good for you, remember me
Eat, eat that spicy food yet think
Of spring-time tunes and honey-bees
I think of you, dear, all the time
My heart weeps day and night
An elephant with but one tusk
Eats lowland grass and soft bamboo
Until the time I see your face
My heart is dark and desolate
An ear of rice, a barley shoot
You are my flower and I'm your bee.

—*Folksong*

The harshness of their native hills forces many Nepali men to seek their living elsewhere and to suffer long partings from those they love back home

Ra-ayo man min ngaich to chu
Fok-ngo el chong chin-min
Ngaich man min re-a-ya to chu
Up pom-cho min ot-koo-po-lon
Ye chu-och ma-ro-vat-chuok
Chap hot chu-el-lon-re-ti
Hom at vach-ngo-min-to-chu
Ngaich chin min, re-ngen meh.

Lok et-chong, chin min ngaich
Koo-po-lon, pom-cho mi-no co-chu
Po-ro-oich ma-ro-vat chuok
Ra-a-yo man min ngaich to-chu
Oich-lok-ngo el ngam mai
Ngaich man min ra-a yo to-chu
Che-he-chon chin-o-re chu-o
To-or ye-chu och hang pul
Op-ha-nam ngem mih no pul
Ngaich chin min, re-ngen meh.

NICOBARESE

Far across the sea, my love

You will be left, my love
        My boat will sail away
You will be all alone
        You must remember me
When I am far away
        Preserve me in your heart
Forget me not, my love
        I have to leave you soon.

Don't cease to think of me
        However far I've sailed
You will be left behind
        I'll be across the sea
I wish I knew a bird
        With wings to fly to you
I wish I was a flower
        The flower that you love best
Do think of me, my love
        I have to leave you soon.

—*Folksong*

A sailor's song from the tropical Nicobarese Islands in the Indian Ocean

स्त्री--आजि त दशहरा पराणधन
वारण करुअछि न जा सदन ।
अनुकूल दिनरे चालित्र जेवे
वर्षकजाक चालुथिवटि तेवे ।
पुरुष—न कर वारण गो पराणसहि
जिवि मातांकु मोर देखिवा पाइँ ।
दाण्डकु वारि माता हेउणथिवे
पुअ आसिव बोलि अनाउथिवे ।
स्त्री—केउँ दिन आसिब मो पाशे फेरि ?
देह मो छुइँ कह न हेव डेरि
वसिण गणुथिवि दिन त मुहिँ
डेरि होइले प्राण रखिबि नाहिँ ।
पुरुष—न कर अविश्वास पराणसहि
कुआँर पुनिअकु आसिबि मुहिँ ।
नव जुवती तुहि वेश होइण
वसिणथिबु वाटकु अनाइण ।

ORIYA

I'll be back

The girl :

Today is Durga Puja day
My darling, please do not go home
If you depart at such a time
You'll be away the whole year long.

The boy :

Please do not try to stop me, dear
I'm going to see my mother now
She's pacing round and round the house
And looks to see which way I'll come.

The girl :

But when will you be back again ?
Touch me and swear it will be soon
I will be counting every day
And if you're late I'll kill myself.

The boy :

My darling, trust me when I swear
The next full moon will see me back
So put your best clothes on, my girl
And watch that day for me to come.

—*Folksong*

Oriya has its own distinctive script, but this folksong is recorded in Devanagari script

په زړه سخت بې مهر یار یې   جفا کار یې دل آزار یې
که هر څو په کوکو ژاړم   ته لا خوښ ځما په کار یې
تا ویشتلي یم فریاد کړم   که خبر په خپل ګذار یې
زه مرهم کړم له تا طمع   ته مِ مالګه دَ پرهار یې
زه به تل ژاړم و تا ته   که ته خوښ ځما په زار یې
زړه دِ وسپاری و غم ته   دَ هغو چه ته دلدار یې
څوک به څه وایي و ما ته   چه یو څه رنګ نګار یې
چه پښپله عاشق وژنې   هم یې ویر کړي په چغار یې
کوم ګناه دَي عاشق کړي   چه یې خیره په ناتار یې
کله درد کله دوا شې   کله خار کله ګلزار یې

په خوشحال دِ غم نازل کړ
چه اغیار سره کنار یې

My tyrant and my torturer

How hard you are, how cruel too
My tyrant and my torturer.

No matter how I weep and wail
To you my pain is just a joke.

You hit me hard, I asked your help
For you should know your blow's effect.

I look to you to soothe my wounds
But you are salt to them instead.

To you will I lament and cry
These cries, I see, are your delight.

Despair and grief alone await
The heart whose worship you command.

For what should I be criticized
When you are quite this beautiful ?

You are your lover's murderer
Who loudly then laments his death.

What has your lover done so wrong
For you to want to plunder him ?

You give me pain, you make me whole
You are my thorn, my rose-bed too.

Oh, how you hurt your poor Khushhal
By keeping others company.

—Khushhal Khan Khatak

A 'ghazal' by a 17th century tribal chieftain

ਮੋਰੀ ਰੁਣਝੁਣ ਲਾਇਆ ਭੈਣੇ ਸਾਵਣੁ ਆਇਆ ।
ਤੇਰੇ ਮੁੰਧ ਕਟਾਰੇ ਜੇਵਡਾ ਤਿਨਿ ਲੋਭੀ ਲੋਭ ਲੁਭਾਇਆ ।
ਤੇਰੇ ਦਰਸਨ ਵਿਟਹੁ ਖੰਨੀਐ ਵੰਞਾ ਤੇਰੇ ਨਾਮ ਵਿਟਹੁ ਕੁਰਬਾਣੋ ।
ਜਾ ਤੂ ਤਾ ਮੈ ਮਾਣੁ ਕੀਆ ਹੈ ਤੁਧੁ ਬਿਨੁ ਕੇਹਾ ਮੇਰਾ ਮਾਣੋ ।
ਚੂੜਾ ਭੰਨੁ ਪਲੰਘ ਸਿਉ ਮੁੰਧੇ ਸਣੁ ਬਾਹੀ ਸਣੁ ਬਾਹਾ ।
ਏਤੇ ਵੇਸ ਕਰੇਦੀਏ ਮੁੰਧੇ ਸਹੁ ਰਾਤੋ ਅਵਰਾਹਾ ।
ਨਾ ਮਨੀਆਰੁ ਨ ਚੂੜੀਆ ਨਾ ਸੇ ਵੰਗੁੜੀਆਹਾ ।
ਜੋ ਸਹ ਕੰਠਿ ਨ ਲਗੀਆ ਜਲਨੁ ਸਿ ਬਾਹੜੀਆਹਾ ।
ਸਭਿ ਸਹੀਆ ਸਹੁ ਰਾਵਣਿ ਗਈਆ ਹਉ ਦਾਧੀ ਕੈ ਦਰਿ ਜਾਵਾ ।
ਅੰਮਾਲੀ ਹਉ ਖਰੀ ਸੁਚਜੀ ਤੈ ਸਹ ਏਕਿ ਨ ਭਾਵਾ ।
ਮਾਠਿ ਗੁੰਦਾਈ ਪਟੀਆ ਭਰੀਐ ਮਾਗ ਸੰਧੂਰੇ ।
ਅਗੈ ਗਈ ਨ ਮੰਨੀਆ ਮਰਉ ਵਿਸੂਰਿ ਵਿਸੂਰੇ ।
ਮੈ ਰੋਵੰਦੀ ਸਭੁ ਜਗੁ ਰੁਨਾ ਰੁੰਨੜੇ ਵਣਹੁ ਪੰਖੇਰੂ ।
ਇਕੁ ਨ ਰੁਨਾ ਮੇਰੇ ਤਨ ਕਾ ਬਿਰਹਾ ਜਿਨਿ ਹਉ ਪਿਰਹੁ ਵਿਛੋੜੀ ।
ਸੁਪਨੈ ਆਇਆ ਭੀ ਗਇਆ ਮੈ ਜਲੁ ਭਰਿਆ ਰੋਇ ।
ਆਇ ਨ ਸਕਾ ਤੁਝ ਕਨਿ ਪਿਆਰੇ ਭੇਜਿ ਨ ਸਕਾ ਕੋਇ ।
ਆਉ ਸਭਾਗੀ ਨੀਦੜੀਏ ਮਤੁ ਸਹੁ ਦੇਖਾ ਸੋਇ ।
ਤੈ ਸਾਹਿਬ ਕੀ ਬਾਤ ਜਿ ਆਖੈ ਕਹੁ ਨਾਨਕ ਕਿਆ ਦੀਜੈ ।
ਸੀਸੁ ਵਢੇ ਕੀਰ ਬੈਸਣੁ ਦੀਜੈ ਵਿਣੁ ਸਿਰ ਸੇਵ ਕਰੀਜੈ ।
ਕਿਉ ਨ ਮਰੀਜੈ ਜੀਅੜਾ ਨਾ ਦੀਜੈ ਜਾ ਸਹੁ ਭਇਆ ਵਿਡਾਣਾ ।

PUNJABI

The rains have arrived

O sister, the rains have arrived and the peacocks are singing
My eyes are like daggers or ropes which will bind him in longing.

Oh how I adore You and worship Your Name !
My pride is for You for without You I'm nothing.

Destroy your rich bedstead and smash up your bracelets
What use is this finery when he loves others ?
You've no one to give you fine bracelets of crystal
What use are your arms if unable to hold Him ?

The girls in my group have all gone to serve Him
But where can I go when nobody wants me ?

My plaits are tied tight and my parting is reddened
Inside though I'm grieving, aware He'll reject me
I weep and my tears make the birds in the wood weep
But dry is this separate pain that's inside me.

You came in a dream once and left me in tears then
I cannot get to You nor can I send someone
Now come to me, sleep, and maybe I'll see Him.

Say, what shall I give to my Lord's message-bearer ?
I'll cut off my head for His seat then I'll serve Him
For life must be offered to end His estrangement.

—*Nanak*

❧ *A lyrical hymn by the first Sikh Guru Nanak (d. 1530), using the Sikh Gurmukhi script* ❧

ہوٹھ سرخ یاقوت جیوں لعل چمکن ٹھوڈی سیب ولایتی سار وچوں
نک الف حسینی دا پپلاسی زلف ناگ خزانے دی بار وچوں
دند چنبے دی لڑی کہ ہنس موتی دانے نکلے حسن انار وچوں
لکھی چین کشمیر تصویر جٹی قد سرو بہشت گلزار وچوں
گردن کونج دی انگلاں رُوانہہ پھلیاں ہتھ کولڑے برگ چنار وچوں
باہاں ویلنے ویلیاں گنھ مکھن چھاتی سنگ مرمر گنگ دھار وچوں
چھاتی ٹھاٹھ دی اُبھری پٹ کھنو سیئو بلخ دے چُنے انبار وچوں
دُھنی بہشت دے حوض دا مُشک قُبہ پیڈو مخملی خاص سرکار وچوں
کافور شاہ سرین بانکے ساق حسن وشتون پہاڑ وچوں
شاہ پری دی بھین پنج پھول رانی گُجھی رہے نہ ہیر ہزار وچوں
متھے آن لگن جہڑے بھور عاشق نکل جان تلوار دی دھار وچوں
عشق بولدا نڈھی دے تھاؤں تھائیں راگ نکلے زیل دی تار وچوں
وارث شاہ جاں نیناں دا داؤ لگے کوئی بچے نہ جُوئے دی ہار وچوں

PUNJABI

She walks in beauty

Her lips are scarlet-red as rubies,
her chin a North-grown apple.
Her locks are snakes, which guard a treasure,
her nose a sharp-edged dagger.
Her teeth are jasmine flowers or petals,
or seeds of pomegranate.
She's a picture from Kashmir or China,
a cypress-tree from heaven.
Her neck a crane's, her fingers pods,
on hands as soft as plane-leaves.
Her arms are soft as butter-pats,
her breast is white as marble.
Her bosoms swell like balls of silk,
choice apples from the North.
Her navel is a musk-filled pool,
her lower belly velvet.
Her well-turned buttocks camphor-white,
her thighs fair-fluted pillars.
A sister to the queen of fairies,
she'd stand out in a thousand.
Her lovers swarm like bees around her,
to sacrifice their being.
For love intones from all her features,
its throbbing treble measures.
When once the eyes take up her challenge,
their stake is lost to start with.

—Varis Shah : 'Hir'

❧ *A description of the heroic from the Muslim romance 'Hir' (1766), using the Persian script* ❧

चालियउ उलगाणउ कातिग मास ।
छोडीया मंदिर घर कबिलास ।
छोडीया चउवारा चउषंडी ।
तठइ पंथ सिरि नयण गमाइया रोइ ।
भूष गई त्रिस ऊचटी ।
कहि न सषीय नींद किसी परि होइ ॥

मगसिरियइ दिन छोटा जी होइ ।
सषीय संदेसउ न पाठवइ कोइ ।
संदेसइ ही बज पडथउ ।
ऊँचा हो परबत नीचा घाट ।
परदेसे पर भुइं गथउ ।
तठइ चीरीय न आवइ न चालए बाट ॥

देषि सषी हिव लागउ छइ पोस ।
धण मरतीय को मत दीयउ दोस ।
दुषि दाधी पंजर हुई ।
धान न भावए तज्या सिरि न्हाण ।
छाहड़ी धूप न आलिंगइ ।
देषतां मंदिर हुयउ मसांण ॥

माह मास इसीय पड़इ ठंठार ।
दाधा छइ बनषंड कीधा हो छार ।
आप दहंती जग दह्यउ ।
म्हाकी चोलीय माहिं थी दाधउ छइ गात्र ।
धणीय बिहूणी धण ताकिजइ ।
तूं तउ उबइगउ रे आविज्यो करह पलाणि ।
जोबन छत्र उमाहियउ ।
म्हाकी कनक काया माहे फेरबी आण ॥

RAJASTHANI

Apart in the winter

November saw the prince set off abroad
He left his palaces, his lofty home
His cupolas and towers.
The princess said with eyes worn out by tears :
'I have no thirst or appetite
My dearest friends, how can I hope to sleep ?'

December saw the days grow short. She said :
'My dearest friends, he sends no word to me
Has lightning burnt his messages ?
He's gone beyond high hills and valleys deep
Away to distant foreign lands
No note or wayfarer brings news of him.

Now January is here, my dearest friends
Do not blame this bride who dies of love !'
Made skeletal by suffering
She cared no more for food or keeping clean.
She thought the sun and shade the same
Her palace in her eyes became a tomb.

Now February came with bitter cold
Consuming all the forest growth.
'I burn—the whole world burns with me !'
She cried : 'Within this dress my body burns
See how she burns without her man—
Saddle your camel, come, come quick
My breasts are firm and fully grown
My golden body's yours to rule !'

—*Narpati Nalha : 'Visaldev-ras'*

From a 15th century example of the popular 'Twelve Month' genre, describing the seasons of love

अिब, सखी, सात वधावा जी म्हा रे आविया
लीना छै आंचळ वार
रँग रो वधावो भँवरजी री कोटड्यां

पहलो वधावो जी म्हां का वाग में
म्हां रो वाग लहरका लेय
आमू तो पाक्या नींबू रस भरया

दूजो वधावो जी भँवरजी रा सहर में
म्हां रे बैठ्या महाजण लोग
हाऱ्यां तो हाऱ्या जी दिवला जुय रह्या

अगणो बधावो भँवरजी री पोळ में
म्हां रे हाती घूमै वार
बांध्या तो तेजी अूभा जव चरै

चौथो वधावो भँवरजी रा चौक में
म्हां रे रुपिया तोरण थांभ
लाडो तो लाडी जी फेरा लै रह्या

पांचवां वधावो भँवरजी री रसोयां
म्हां रे गरड़ो पड़ै छै रसोय
दुध तो कढै छै घ्रत मावटै

छठो वधावो भँवरजी रा महल में
म्हां रो महल रह्यो गरणाय
अजब झरोखा जी छाजा झुक रह्या

सातवों वधावो भँवरजी री सेज में
म्हां रे बैठ्या राज-दिवाण
ढोलो तो मारूणी हँस वतळावसी

RAJASTHANI

The seven blessings

O my friend, seven blessings have come to our house
To receive them I've spread out the edge of my veil
To the home of my husband great blessings have come.

The first's my garden which waves in the breeze
Where the mangoes are ripe and there's juice in the limes.

The second is in the fair town of my love
Where rich merchants are sitting with lights in their shops.

The next one is outside my dear husband's gate
Where the elephant sways and the horse feeds in peace.

The fourth is within my dear husband's court
Where the groom and the bride will go round the pole.

The fifth is within that kitchen of his
Where the Brahmins are cooking with butter and milk.

The sixth is within that palace of his
Where the windows and balconies sound and smell sweet.

The seventh is found in my dear husband's bed
Where together in love we both laugh as we talk.

—*Women's folksong*

❧ *This song is unusual for its touching celebration of a happy marriage* ❧

Bonero pakhia kande
Bhinu bhinu kande piari.

Mach kande ghumure ghumur piari
Pran kande tomari lagi.

Car konia pukhuri
Nana ronger pahkir basa he.

Khanek nuṙe khanek boṣe
Basa nạhi pae khujiya pae ?

❧

Jolke ba gele biṭi
Kene ba biṭi pallum ?

Ki ba mai bolibo
Ki ba mai kohibo ?

Rajaram bagane
Phula phuṭilo.

Se o phul ṭuṭite
Amae topol holo !

SANTALI

Where are their nests ?

The birds in the wood are crying, my love
Crying their different songs.

How softly the fish too are crying, my love
Listen, my soul cries for you.

See how at each of the water's four corners
Bright-coloured birds have their nests.

Some fly in the sky and some perch on the branches
Where are their nests, though ? Oh, where are their nests ?

❧

So why did you go to the water, my girl ?
So why did you run away from me, my girl ?

Dear mother, what can I tell you ?
Dear mother, what can I say then ?

In Rajaram's garden
The flowers are blooming.

The bushes that bloom there
Have seized me so tightly !

—*Two folksongs*

❧ Vivid tribal songs of the Santal people of North-Eastern India ❧

ڪاتي تکي م ٿئي، مر منيائي هوءِ،
مان ورمني توهه، مون پريان جا هٿڙا.

جي تون سگهين سگهيو، ته ڪاتيءَ ٿي م ڪنجهه،
سپيريان جي سور جو، ماڙهن ڏجي نه منجهه،
آندر ايءَ آهنج، سانڍج سڪائون ڪري.

اصل عاشقن جو، سر نه سانڍڻ ڪم،
سؤ سيسناڻ آڪرو، سندو دوساڻ دم،
هيءَ هڏو ۾ جم، پک پرياڻ جيءَ نه پڙي.

منڌ پيندي مون، ساڄن سهي سڃاتو.
بي پيالو عشق جو، سيڪي سمجهوسون،
ساڄن سهي سڃاتو.
پريان سندي پار جي، آندر آگ آئئون،
ساڄن سهي سڃاتو.
جيئن ناهي جڳ ۾، ڏينهن مڙهئي ڏون،
ساڄن سهي سڃاتو.
آلا! عبداللطيف چئي، آهين توئهين تون،
ساڄن سهي سڃاتو.

SINDHI

Witnessing true love

I hope the knife He holds is blunt, not sharp
His hand must thus stay longer on my flesh.

❦

No lover should complain about His knife
Or publicly disclose the pain He brings
With firm intent retain your hurt within.

❀

No real lovers rate their lives above
A single breath of their Beloved or
Their skin and bones above His drop of spit.

❦

I've drunk up the wine
        I've witnessed my Love
I've drunk passion's cup
I've understood all
        I've witnessed my Love
For His sake I'm happy
These flames should consume me
        I've witnessed my Love
Our life in this world
Lasts hardly two days
        I've witnessed my Love
Says Abdul Latif :
It's You who exist
        I've witnessed my Love.

—Shah Abdul Latif

❧ *Sufi verses from the Risalo, the great Sindhi classic by Shah Abdul Latif (d. 1752)* ❧

නී බෝ   දෙවඟනක මෙන් දිලෙන හැම ස   ද
සු බෝ   පබාවත් ලඳගෙන් වෙන්ව ග   ද
නොබෝ   කල් පසුව ගිය සඳෙහි දුක් වැ   ද
එ බෝ   සත් කුසා රජ තාන් යහණි ඉ   ද

නු බ ප ත   සඳ යුගත රිවි ලෙස දි   ස් වි ය
ය හ ණ ත   අතුළ මල් පෙති කටු මෙල   ස් වී ය
පි ය ක ත   දෙන රුඟුම් ගී නොම තො   ස් වී ය
ප බ ව ත   නැතී මෙ රජ විමනත හී   ස් වී ය

නි ම ල්   වතිත් විහිදෙන සිනිඳු සොම් තැලු   ම්
සු පු ල්   ර්ණ ලියක මෙන් දිලෙන වත දූගු   ම්
ල ක ල්   පබාවති රජ දූ සමග උතු   ම්
කි ක ල්   ලැබේ දෙ එක යහණතේ ලැගු   ම්

සි හි ල්   සොම් තරිඳු රිවි මෙන් දි   සේ යා
කොමුල්   නද ඇසෙයි යකු හඬ මෙලි   සේ යා
ල ක ල්   පබාවති සහ නොම වැ   සේ යා
මෙ කල්   මෙමා සිතු නලවම් කෙ   සේ යා

සු නී ල්   නෙතිඳුවර බැම බිඟු වත කම   ලා
වි පු ල්   තන තිසර සපිරුණු පැහැ සිලී   ලා
නි ම ල්   පබාවතී තුනු විලෙගි මනක   ලා
කි ක ල්   ගිලී කෙළිම් ද වඩමිනි ලො   ලා

හැ ම ස ත්   ඝෝර සසර සයුරෙන් ගොඩ නඟ   න
ඇ ති ව ත්   පුන් පෙරුම් මතු බුදු බව ලබ   න
ප බ ව ත්   වෙන්වුවෙත් නැතිවම ඉඳැ යහ   ණ
ම හ ස ත්   තැමුනු ලෙස මම කියම් කෙලෙසි   න

SINHALA

The Bodhisattva's lament

The royal Bodhisattva lay
Alone, quite overcome by grief
To find himself forsaken by
His goddess-bright Prabhavati.

'Without my bride, this palace and
Its dancing-girls give me no joy
This bed we shared feels sharp as thorns
This moon a life-consuming sun.

When shall I hold my love again
And sleep with my beloved bride
Whose face's light shone sweet and soft
Like golden flowers upon the vine ?

The moon now blazes like the sun
The birdsongs grate like demon yells
How can my heart be comforted
When my Prabhavati is gone ?

My love is like a crystal pool
Her breasts its gliding snow-white swans
Her eyes a lotus, her brows two bees
Her face a lily . . . where has she gone ?'

Such was the agonizing pain
Inflicted by Prabhavati
Upon the Lord who later would
As Buddha grant us all release !

—*Alagiyavanna : 'Kusada-kava'*

❧ *From a 17th century Sri Lankan poem about the Buddha's 534th pre-manifestation as a king whose ugliness repelled his bride* ❧

وچ روہی دے رہندیاں　　نازک نازو جٹیاں

راتیں کرن شکار دلیندے　　ڈیہاں ولوڑن مٹیاں

گجھڑے تیر چلاون کاری　　سے سے دلڑیاں پھٹیاں

کر کر دردمنداں کوں زخمی　　ہے ہے بدھن نہ پٹیاں

چھیڑن بھیڈاں بکریاں گائیں　　لیلے گابے کٹیاں

کئی مسکین مسافر پھاتھے　　چوڑ کیتو نے ترٹیاں

ڈہوئیں وار فقیر ٹھیو سے　　فخر وڈایاں سٹیاں

ہیوں دلبر دے کنڑے در دے　　برہوں پیاں گل گٹیاں

مونجھ فرید مرید ہمیشہ　　اج کلھ خوشیاں گھٹیاں

Siraiki

The desert girls

Out in the desert sands there roam
The lovely tribal girls.

By night they hunt for lovers' hearts
They churn their pots by day.

They fire their secret deadly darts
And many hearts they wound.

The hurts of those whom they attack
Remain, alas, undressed.

They drive their sheep and goats and cows
Their lambs and kids and calves.

All travellers who cross their path
Are caught and quite destroyed.

A desert maid has humbled me
To beg like a fakir.

A dog before her door I lie
With longing as my leash.

A deeper sadness grows on me
My happy times are gone.

—*Khwaja Ghulam Farid*

❧ *A Sufi song by Khwaja Ghulam Farid (d. 1901) whose desert sweetheart became his second wife* ❧

باغاں وچ گھا کوئی ناں
جیہڑے پاسے ماہی ٹُریا
اوں پاسے داراہ کوئی ناں

بدلی آگئی ہے ساوݨ دی
کوئی تدبیر ڈَسا
رُٹھے یار مناوݨ دی

دریا وِچ بیڑی ہے
رُلی ہوئی قسمت چا
اللہ پاک نکھیڑی ہے

باغاں وچ انب جھُلدے
سجݨ سیانے ہوندے
اساں دردر کیوں رُلدے

سونے دے ترے ماسے
کیں چاجگایا ہے
تیڈی یادوچ پئے ہاسے

کوئی لمبوں جہاز آیا
سُتیاں دیاں اُکھڑگئیاں
کوئی ویلا جو یاد آیا!

چاٹے وِچ سپ ہوندا
اِنہاں کوں توں کون رُسے
جنہاں باجھ نہ جھٹ پوندا

SIRAIKI

The garden's bare of grass

The garden's bare of grass—
Where did my lover go ?
I see no track or pass.

❦

With clouds the sky is black—
Explain to me a plan
To win my lover back.

❀

The ship sails on the sea—
Our fates were one till God
Set you apart from me.

❦

The mangos grow so sweet—
If he was more aware
Why should I roam this street ?

❀

Three grains of gold will do—
Who rudely made me wake
From my sweet dreams of you ?

❦

A boat came from the south—
A sudden special thought
Left me with open mouth.

❀

The snake writhes in the net—
Who can be cross with him
Without whom I'm upset ?

—*Anonymous*

❧ *Examples of the 'mahiya' verse form, whose evocative first line rhymes with the third* ❧

திரைவிரி தருதுறையே திருமணல் விரியிடமே
விரைவிரி நறுமலரே மிடைதரு பொழிலிடமே
மருவிரி புரிகுழலே மதிபுரை திருமுகமே
யிருகய லிணைவிழியே யெனையிடர் செய்தவையே.
வளைவளர் தருதுறையே மணம்விரி தருபொழிலே
தளையவிழ் நறுமலரே தனியவ டிரியிடமே
முளைவள ரிளநகையே முழுமதி புரைமுகமே
யிளையவ ளிணைமுலையே யெனையிடர் செய்தவையே.

பவள வுலக்கை கையாற் பற்றித்
தவள முத்தங் குறுவாள் செங்கண்
தவள முத்தங் குறுவாள் செங்கண்
குவளை யல்ல கொடிய கொடிய.
புன்னை நீழற் புலவுத் திரைவா
யன்ன நடப்ப நடப்பாள் செங்க
ணன்ன நடப்ப நடப்பாள் செங்கண்
கொன்னே வெய்ய கூற்றங் கூற்றம்.
கள்வாய் நீலங் கையி னேந்திப்
புள்வா யுணங்கல் கடிவாள் செங்கண்
புள்வா யுணங்கல் கடிவாள் செங்கண்
வெள்வே லல்ல வெய்ய வெய்ய.

TAMIL

Thinking of her beside the sea

These breaking waves, this beach, these shining sands
These scented flowers, this grove beside the sea
Her fragrant hair, bright face and carp-like eyes
All these have brought distress to me

These conch-shells on the shore, these fragrant groves
These tender petals, these secret haunts of hers
Her fresh young teeth, bright face and youthful breasts
All these have brought distress to me.

❦

How red are the eyes of the girl who is using
Her pestle of coral to pound the white pearls
How red are her eyes, no dark lilies are they
So cruel, so cruel . . .

How red are the eyes of the girl who is swaying
Along like a swan in the grove by the shore
How red are her eyes as she sways like a swan
Like death, like death . . .

How red are the eyes of the girl who is scaring
The birds from the fish with sweet flowers in her hand
How red are her eyes as she scares off the birds
So cruel, so cruel . . .

—Ilanko Atikal : 'Cilappatikaram'

❧ *Vivid lyrics from the romantic epic 'Cilappatikaram' (c. 300 AD), attributed to the Jain prince Ilanko* ❧

இல்லை தவறவர்க் காயினு மூடுதல்
வல்ல தவரளிக்கு மாறு.

ஊடலிற் றோன்றுஞ் சிறுதுனி நல்லளி
வாடினும் பாடு பெறும்.

தவறில ராயினுந் தாமவீழ்வார் மென்றோ
ளகறலி னாங்கொன் றுடைத்து.

உணலினு முண்ட தறலினிது காமம்
புணர்தலி னூட லினிது.

ஊடலிற் றோற்றவர் வென்றா ரதுமன்னும்
கூடலிற் காணப் படும்.

ஊடிப் பெறுகுவங் கொல்லோ நுதல்வெயர்ப்பக்
கூடலிற் றோன்றிய வுப்பு.

ஊடுக மன்னோ வொளியிழை யாமிரப்ப
நீடுக மன்னோ விரா.

ஊடுதல் காமத்திற் கின்ப மதற்கின்பங்
கூடி முயங்கப் பெறின்.

TAMIL

Lovers' quarrels

He may be sweet and innocent—but still
A show of jealousy won't hurt.

❦

A quarrel's sharp but passing pain will soon
Rejuvenate a love grown stale.

❧

To be refused a kiss when not at fault
Can have its own particular charm.

❀

To pause while eating makes the food taste sweet
Quarrels improve the taste of love.

❦

The loser wins in lovers' quarrellings
Who most enjoys their making up ?

❧

Shall we enjoy again the happiness
Produced by her pretended rage ?

❀

Be angry then—so long as I have time
To plead my case to you this night.

❦

It is through quarreling that lovers grow
Together in sweet harmony.

—Tiruvalluvar : 'Tirukkural'

❧ *The final verses from the great Tamil book of wisdom composed around 400 AD* ❧

தம்மமர் காதலர் தார்சூழ் அணிஅகலம்
விம்ம முயங்குந் துணையில்லார்க் — கிம்மெனப்
பெய்ய எழிலி முழங்குந் திசையெல்லாம்
நெய்தல் அறைந்தன்ன நீர்த்து.

கம்மஞ்செய் மாக்கள் கருவி ஒடுக்கிய
மம்மர்கொண் மாலை மலர்ஆய்ந்து பூத்தொடுப்பாள்
கைம்மாலை இட்டுக் கலுழ்ந்தா டுணையில்லார்க்
கிம்மாலை என்செய்வ தென்று.

ஓலைக் கணக்கர் ஒலிஅடங்கு’ புன்செக்கர்
மாலைப் பொழுதின் மணந்தார் பிரிவுள்ளி
மாலை பரிந்திட் டழுதாள், வனமுலைமேல்
கோலஞ்செய் சாந்தந் திமிர்ந்து.

செல்சுடர் நோக்கிச் சிதரரிக்கண் கொண்டநீர்
மெல்விரல் ஊழ்தெறியா விம்மித்தன் — மெல்விரலின்
நாள்வைத்து நங்குற்றம் எண்ணுங்கொல் அந்தோதன்
தோள்வைத் தணைமேற் கிடந்து?

Scenes of separation

With bodies decked with flowers they once enjoyed
Love's close embrace, but now these heavy rains
Bring a thunder that recalls the funeral drum
They so miss their lover's company . . .

❦

As evening fell and workmen downed their tools
She picked some flowers to make herself a wreath
But then he let her garland fall and cried :
'How will this help my lonely tears ?'

❀

As scholars laid aside their palm-leaf scrolls
And twilight fell, she sadly thought of him
She pulled the flowers from her wreath and wiped
The fragrant sandal from her breast.

❧

As sunset glows she wipes each tear away
With those same fingers which she uses to
Count off the days he has been gone, while he
Thinks : 'Is she counting up my faults ?'

–'Naladiyar'

❧ *Quatrains from the 'Naladiyar', a Jain collection assembled soon after the 'Tirukkural'* ❧

తొడల మెరుపు జూచి, తోరంపు కుచములు,
వార కొప్పు గలుగు వనిత జూచి,
విటుడు నిలుచునె’ ట్లు, విరహా’ గ్ని జొరకను?

ఎర్రదానివాడు నేపా’ ర ఁజూచిన,
వేకి ఁబుట్టి చాల వెర్రి ఁబట్టు,
పల్లు ఁదెరచి నగిన, ఁబట్టు పెన్భూతంబు.

ఎట్టి స్త్రీల గనినని’ ంతంత యన రాదు,
కాలవహ్ని లక్క గరగిన’ ట్లు,
యిట్టి గాఢ మోహ మె’ ంతైన జేయురా!

కూడు గుడిచి లెస్స కూర్చున్న వాడైన
నాడు దాని ఁగన్న న’ ట్టె తగులు,
న’ న్న రసమ, యొడలిక’ తి మదంబ’ గు సుమీ.

అన్న - మదమువలనన’ తివలు’ నరుల’ ట్టు
లే’ పు రేగి, మదనుడే’ చెన’ ందు
ర;’ న్నము’ డుగు వెనుకన’ తడె’ ందు ఁబోయెరా!

వలపు ఁదీరనే’ ని, వనజాక్షి యధరంబు
ములక - పంటి గిజరు, ముష్టి రసము,
చింత లేని వేళ, జీడి - సమానమో

TELUGU

Beginnings and endings

When he beholds the beauty of her form
And sees the wavings of her waist-long hair
What man resists a lovely woman's charms ?

❦

Simply to see a lovely woman thrills
Us with a fever sure to drive us mad—
Her teeth flashed in a smile are something else !

❀

Can men who stare at women know them as
They truly are ? Desire destroys their sense
Dissolving them like gum that melts in flames.

❦

A man who has feasted and sits at his ease
Has feelings of love at the sight of a woman
For food is the force which inflames his desire.

❀

Both men and women when well-filled with food
Will say that Cupid is tormenting them
But empty stomachs make love powerless.

❦

When love is past, those cherry lips taste like
The nightshade's berry or the poison-nut
Old passion's like the acid mango-leaf.

—*Vemana*

❧ *Vemana (c. 1500) is supposed to have been a one-time pleasure-lover who turned ascetic* ❧

ایک دن فرش پر تھا میرا ہاتھ
باتیں کرتے تھے وے بھی میرے ساتھ
پانوں سے ایک اُنگلی مل ڈالی
لطف سے درد وہ نہ تھا خالی
درد سے کی جو میں نے بیتابی
دستِ نازک سے دیر تک دابی
یاد آتے ہیں ایسے لطف جواب
گزرے ہیں جانِ غم زدہ پہ غضب
تن بدن دیکھ جی نہ رہتا تھا
میں جو گستاخ ہو کے کہتا تھا
کہ یہ جاگہ تم اس فقیر کو دو
متبسم ہو کہتے وے یہ لو
یہ بھی کیا کیا خیال رکھتے ہیں
آرزوے محال رکھتے ہیں
پھر گھڑی بھر میں کہتے ہو نہ ملول
مار کھانے کی باتیں سب ہیں قبول
جب سلوک ان کو یاد آتا ہے
کیا کہوں جی ہی بھول جاتا ہے

ایک دن پان وے چباتے تھے
سُرخ لب اُن کے مجھکو بھاتے تھے
کہہ اُٹھا میں اگر اُگال سے مجھے
مُنھ سے دو تو کرو نہال مجھے
بولے یوں نہیں ہے میں کہا ہاں سچ
جھوٹا کھاتے ہیں میٹھے کی لالچ
ہنس کے اُس وقت مجھ کو ٹال دیا
پھر اُسی رنگ سے اُگال دیا
ایسی صد رنگ مہربانی تھی
تب سیہ رو کی زندگانی تھی
ایسے سے رنگ گر فلک لاتا
خاک کے رنگ میں مجھے پاتا

Memories of intimacy

One day my hand was lying on the ground
As we were talking to each other, when
She crushed my finger with her foot and gave
Me pain not empty of delight, and when
I shrieked in agony she massaged it
With long and gentle strokes. (How hard it is
For me now to recall those pleasures past !)
The sight of her would be too much for me
And I would boldly ask : 'Give me this bit !'
She'd smile and say : 'Well, take it, here you are.
I see forbidden fancies fill your brain !'
Without a moment's sadness was I then
Ready to suffer anything from her.
When now I think of her behaviour to me—
What can I say ?—I'm overwhelmed by thoughts . . .

One day as she was sitting chewing *paan*
I loved the betel's redness on her lips
And burst out saying : 'If you'd squirt the juice
From your mouth into mine, how glad I'd be !'
'No way !' she said, but I replied : 'How sweet
I'd find the taste of what you've chewed and left !'
She laughed, first put me off, then passed to me
Her lovely leavings. In such gentle ways
As these was she so often kind until
Dark destiny wiped colour from my life.

—Mir Taqi Mir : 'Mu'amalat-e Ishq'

From an 18th century autobiographical poem by the greatest of the Urdu love-poets

دلِ ناداں تجھے ہوا کیا ہے؟
آخر اِس درد کی دوا کیا ہے؟

ہم ہیں مشتاق اور وہ بیزار
یا الٰہی یہ ماجرا کیا ہے؟

میں بھی منہ میں زبان رکھتا ہوں
کاش پوچھو کہ مدّعا کیا ہے؟

جب کہ تجھ بن نہیں کوئی موجود
پھر یہ ہنگامہ اے خدا کیا ہے؟

یہ پری چہرہ لوگ کیسے ہیں؟
غمزہ و عشوہ و ادا کیا ہے؟

شکنِ زلفِ عنبریں کیوں ہے؟
نگہِ چشمِ سرمہ سا کیا ہے؟

سبزہ و گل کہاں سے آئے ہیں؟
ابر کیا چیز ہے؟ ہوا کیا ہے؟

ہم کو اُن سے وفا کی ہے امّید
جو نہیں جانتے، وفا کیا ہے؟

ہاں بھلا کر، ترا بھلا ہو گا
اَور درویش کی صدا کیا ہے؟

جان تم پر نثار کرتا ہوں
میں نہیں جانتا، دعا کیا ہے؟

میں نے مانا کہ کچھ نہیں غالبؔ!
مفت ہاتھ آئے تو بُرا کیا ہے؟

What is all this ?

What ails you, my foolish heart ?
Does this pain have any cure ?

I am eager and she is cool
O God, what is all this ?

I too possess a tongue,
Just ask what I desire !

When none but You exists,
O God, what is this turmoil ?

What are these fairy folk,
Their graces, airs and charms ?

Why these twisting scented locks ?
Why this glancing made-up eye ?

Whence have come the rose and verdure ?
What is a cloud, what the breeze ?

We hope for faith from her
Who does not know its meaning !

'Do good that you may prosper !'
Is this poor beggar's cry.

I sacrifice my life for you,
What else is prayer to me ?

Ghalib is worth nothing, sure,
But free, so why complain ?

—*Ghalib*

Perhaps the best known of all Urdu 'ghazals', by the famous Urdu poet Ghalib (d. 1869)

اٹھتی ہیں تو لوگ بسم اللہ کہتے ہیں ،
چلتی ہیں تو لوگ آنکھیں بچھاے دیتے ہیں، یہ ہیں کہ کسی کی پرواہی نہیں کرتیں ، جو ہے انھیں کے حکم کا تابع ہے ،حکومت بھی وہ کہ زمین و آسمان ٹل جاے مگر ان کا کہنا نہ ٹلے ۔ فرمایشوں کا تو ذکر ہی کیا،بن مانگے لوگ کلیجہ نکال نکال کے دیے دیتے ہیں ۔ کوئی دل ہتھیلی پر رکھے ہوئے ہے کوئی جان قربان کرتا ہے ۔یہاں کسی کی نذر ہی قبول نہیں ہوتی ۔ کوئی بات نظر میں نہیں سماتی ۔ بے پروائی یہ کہ کوئی جان بھی دے دے تو ان کے نزدیک کوئی مال نہیں ۔ غرور ایسا کہ ہفت اقلیم کی سلطنت اُن کی ٹھوکر پہ ہے ۔ ناز وہ جو کسی سے اٹھایا نہ جاے مگر اٹھانے والے اٹھاتے ہیں ۔ انداز وہ جو مار ہی ڈالے مگر مرنے والے مرہی جاتے ہیں ۔ اِدھر اس کو رلا دیا اُدھر اسے ہنسا دیا ۔ کسی کے کلیجے میں چٹکی لے لی ۔ کسی کا دل تلووں سے مَل ڈالا ۔ بات بات میں روٹھی جاتی ہیں ۔ لوگ منا رہے ہیں ۔ کوئی ہاتھ جوڑ رہا ہے کوئی منت کر رہا ہے ۔ قول کیا اور مکر گئیں ۔ قسم کھائی اور بھول گئیں ۔ محفل بھر میں سب کی نگاہ ان کی طرف ہے ، یہ آنکھ اٹھا کے بھی نہیں دیکھتیں پھر جدھر دیکھ لیا ادھر سب دیکھنے لگے ۔ جس پر ان کی نگاہ پڑتی ہے اس پر ہزاروں نگاہیں پڑتی ہیں ۔ رشک کے مارے لوگ جلے جاتے ہیں اور یہ جان جان کے جلا رہی ہیں اور لطف یہ کہ دل میں کچھ نہیں وہ بھی ہیچ یہ بھی ہیچ ہے ۔ فقط بناوٹ ۔ اگر وہ بیچارہ اس فریب میں آگیا پھر کیا تھا پہلے بظاہر خود مرنے لگیں سہ

آج کل اُن کو بہت ہے مری خاطر منظور
یا مری یا مرے دشمن کی قضا آئی ہے

Cruel courtesans

When the courtesans stood up, their beauty made men invoke God. When they walked, people laid glances for them to walk on. But they cared for nobody and treated everyone as a slave. Such was their power that heaven and earth might move but their word was absolute. They had no need to demand, since men would give them their hearts and sacrifice their lives to them without being asked. But they accepted no gifts and attended to no requests, being so indifferent that the gift of a man's life was of little account to them. They were so arrogant that they would trample with contempt on the offer of the greatest empire in the world. Their whims might be impossible, but there were always some admirers who would try to gratify them. Their coquetry might be fatal, but there were plenty willing to die. They would make one man weep, then another laugh. They would tweak one man's heart, then trample on another's. They would become sulky at the slightest pretext. Their admirers would try to appease them with coaxing words and humbly folded hands, but they would take not the slightest notice. They would agree to make up, but then go back on their word. They would solemnly swear to grant some favour, but then forget all about it. All eyes would be upon them, but they would not deign to glance back. All eyes turned in whichever direction they looked, and all eyes glowered on any upon whom their eyes rested. Men were consumed with jealousy and they deliberately fed the flames. But in their hearts all they felt was contempt. It was all a show in which they would at first pretend to be in love with any poor wretch who fell for their tricks.

> Today she is so sweet and kind to me—
> Who is to die : my rival or myself ?

—*Rusva : 'Umrao Jan Ada'*

❧ *An extract from a 19th century novel mirroring the opening Kamasutra quotation written 1,500 years earlier* ❧

Proverbs of Love

'If there is love,
the impossible
becomes possible.'

Assamese

The kiss of love breaks the nose.
Short women are like worn-out brooms.
A hasty cook and a hasty broom, the husband goes fasting; a slow cook and a slow broom, the husband eats three meals a day.
In the home the wife is supreme, in the ditch the water sprite reigns.
She has not a hair on the crown of her head, yet her husband still calls her beautiful.
To seek turtle eggs in the mountains, to dam a stream in the flat-plains—these are as difficult to do as for a widower to keep a dry field.
She who has no baby to dandle should make her old man dance.
She cut off her own nose to prevent her husband's second wife from starting her journey.

Bengali

When the heart clings to a lover, who cares whether he be a low-caste *Hari* or *Dom* ?
An unchaste mistress is her slavegirl's servant.
Sin through lust and death through sin !
The husband is no husband to his wife, but sworn brother-in-law to the courtesan.
A deceiver's love is like a razor's edge—there is no regard for any, when any may be gained by unfaithfulness.
Sweet mouths gain heart's wishes.

Hindi

Your beauty's in your food, your grace in your clothes.
Love, a cough and an itch are three things that cannot be hidden.
A woman's first counsel is good.
The happy wife is she whose husband asks no questions.
Make your home in someone's heart.
The eyes love beauty, the heart loves wisdom.
Stolen sugar is sweetest !

When a couple breaks up, a piece is lost.
She who is born beautiful is born married.
If there's a place in the heart, there'll be a place in the home.
The love of a foreigner warms like a bonfire of loose grass.
Who bites the cheek on the very first kiss ?
Love and power never seek to be shared.
If kept up, it is love; if not, it is dirt.
When the queen is offended, she'll take back her jewels.
Beauty weeps while luck enjoys.
Even a *houri* as co-wife is worse than a witch.

KASHMIRI

Love and dust cannot be hid.
A woman's laugh is her go-between with her man.
He fell in the mud with his heart on the weeds.
The one-eyed girl got her man but not a room in which to sleep with him.
Bachelors long for it and married men regret it.
A quarrel between husband and wife is like a monsoon shower.
An old man's love is worth a guinea a pinch.
'How is your second husband, O mother ?' 'Better by far than begging !'

KUMAONI

A woman will remain chaste herself and not at her father's command.
When a woman shows her teeth and speaks, a man finds her motive.
An hour of misery is equal to a hundred hours of pleasure.
Seeing his wife naked and that of another well-clothed and adorned, the man says his father was a fool since he did not marry the other woman to him.
The lovers of your wife and pebbles in your shoe will always trouble you.
Sunstroke on a cloudy day is as unexpected as the blow dealt by a lover.

The mother cries for her daughter, the daughter for her lover and the lover for his own family.

Ladakhi

The *shava* deer walking in the hills is a delight for the eye, a fine girl walking in the street is a delight for the heart.

Marathi

A husband is good if he gives a good nose-ring.

Forehead powder for a widow and *kātabola* medicine for a barren woman—both are useless.

The widow bathed but the water was wasted.

Call me a widow or whatever you will, but at least give me enough to eat.

For a married woman there is only her own house or her father's.

One fair woman—and she has seventy-two hidden vices.

Bear the pain of labour once and become mistress of the house.

She who has one child cries, she who has two cries, she who has seven cries, and she who has none . . . she also cries.

Another man's wife is a poisonous plant.

Women's wisdom is linked to the hearth.

Women are attracted by rich men.

Nepali

Where there is a woman, there is prosperity.

What takes a year for a man to do takes but a moment for a woman.

The quarrel between a man and his wife is like a straw on fire.

The man with two wives sits in a corner and cries.

The first wife asks for rain, the second for the sun, so where shall I, an old man, go ?

The pot of your co-wife is always larger.

Only money in your hand and your wife in sight belong to you.

The woman who loves ten different men has no one when she is about to die.

Newari

A man who has not travelled and a woman who has not given birth are alike.
A beautiful woman is unfortunate.
A beautiful woman may not remain faithful.
While the couple quarrels, the monkey picks up the fruit.
A friend who comes to smoke with you may steal your wife.
Love begets sorrow.
The mother makes eyes, the daughter hugs in the street.

Pashto

Advice is wasted on lovers.
An old man making love to a maiden is like a Hindu riding a cow.

Punjabi

The one who feels it knows—who knows another's pain ?
Never mix love and business.
Women who have drunk from love's cup are no good for housework.
Once plucked, the petals of the heart cannot be put back.
Hearts are deeper than the ocean—who knows their secrets ?
The way to a heart is through other hearts.
A woman's heart is like a glass ring.
Love cannot be won by force.
The path of love is never smooth.
Love's ways are strange.
Love is blind.
Does love have a religion ?

Sindhi

If money is in plenty, love is at hand.
Love makes no distinction between a good caste and a bad one.
An old husband for a young wife is like an arrow in her side.
No use marrying an old man and wasting life, for while the wheat crops are reaped he may break down.

O heart, love me so that I may love you.
She sulks with her husband but ignores the whole village.
Women are the food of women.
This is not love but an affliction !
The young wife lives off the earnings of her husband but says 'May my father love long !'
When betrothed, he is entangled, when married he is in stocks—silence people ! Man and money are both lost.
Better a heated heel than a heated heart.

Tamil

Though there is no fault in him, the sweet way he expresses his love has the power to create jealous petulance.
The pain created by a quarrel of lovers will tone drooping happiness and cause it to bloom once more.
Though free from fault, being released from the embracing arms of your beloved has its own unique charm.
In love, a lovers' quarrel is sweeter than reunion.
In a lovers' quarrel, the one who seems to lose is the one who wins in the end. This is clear from the joy of reunion.
Let her with bright jewels display her anger more and more—let me plead with her more and more to appease her. Let the night last long enough to give me the chance for this !
Lovers' quarrels make their love sweet. Thus love derives its happiness. When lovers embrace, their hearts are united in harmony.
A character full of love is like a river without a wave.
If there is love, the impossible becomes possible.
Love is all-important—and it is its own reward.
One who is not melted by anything may be melted by passion.
Love is like the needle attracted to the magnet.
Just as a flood cannot carry off the melt water, no outside force can destroy love.
Whoever the Rajah praises becomes the nymph Ramba.
Trees, forest and all seem to be her.

Telugu

They eat from one dish and sleep on one bed.
He called the woman he could not get as a wife a harlot.
Look at the mother before you take her daughter—see how much milk the buffalo gives before you buy her.
A laughing woman and a crying man should not be trusted.
One act of adultery does away with a hundred good deeds.
When he arrived at the marriage feast, she had already begun enquiring how the bridegroom was related to her.
If given with love, a handful is sufficient.
Even the goddess of pestilence passes over the woman unloved by her husband.
Even if Cupid himself were the husband of a bad woman, still she would not give up her evil practices.
She who has taken lovers and she who has eaten the skin of boiled milk will never cease doing so.
An old man is fond of women.

Urdu

Love and musk cannot be hidden, however hard you try.
One heart is another's delight.
Love destroys modesty.
Love is without law.
In love a king and beggars are equal.
Let love be long however little.
Majnun loved both Leila and her dog.
What is a fairy to one who has fallen for a donkey ?
A woman who laughs is half won.
When love is over, all their faults are revealed.
Being a lover is not like being at your aunt's house.

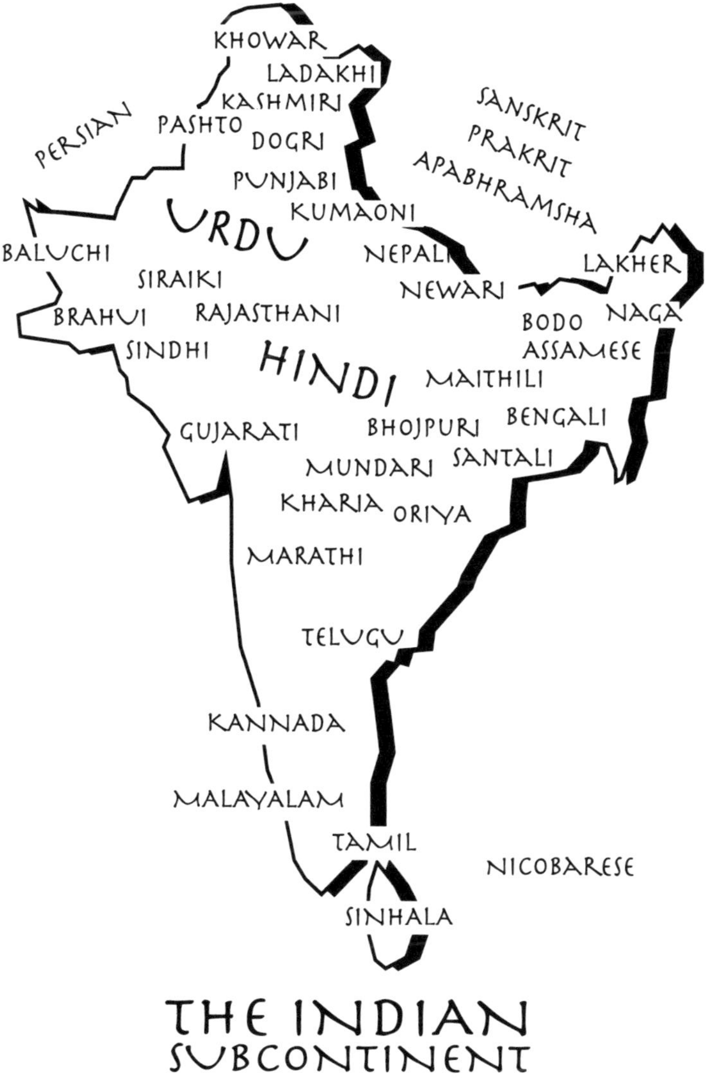
KHOWAR
LADAKHI
KASHMIRI
PASHTO
PERSIAN
DOGRI
PUNJABI
SANSKRIT
PRAKRIT
APABHRAMSHA
URDU
KUMAONI
BALUCHI
NEPALI
LAKHER
SIRAIKI
NEWARI
BRAHUI
RAJASTHANI
BODO
NAGA
SINDHI
HINDI
ASSAMESE
MAITHILI
GUJARATI
BHOJPURI
BENGALI
MUNDARI
SANTALI
KHARIA
ORIYA
MARATHI
TELUGU
KANNADA
MALAYALAM
TAMIL
NICOBARESE
SINHALA
THE INDIAN
SUBCONTINENT

Index of Poets & Works